Voluntary Service Overseas

Voluntary Service Overseas

The Story of the First Ten Years

Michael Adams

With a Foreword by
H.R.H. PRINCE PHILIP
Duke of Edinburgh

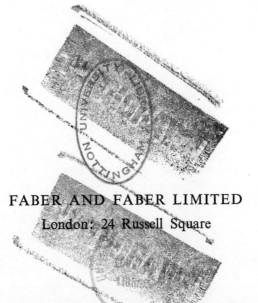

FABER AND FABER LIMITED
London: 24 Russell Square

First published in 1968
by Faber and Faber Limited
London, 24 Russell Square
Printed in Great Britain by
Billing & Sons Limited, Guildford, Surrey

SBN (hard bound edition) 571 08323 4
SBN (paper bound edition) 571 08337 4

831120

c

Foreword

by H.R.H. Prince Philip, Duke of Edinburgh

The first time I heard about what was to become Voluntary Service Overseas was during a visit to Sarawak in 1959. Two or three boys, who had just left school and had a year to wait before they could get a place at University, were teaching in village schools. I thought it was a splendid idea and I remember thinking at the time that like all really good ideas it was so essentially simple. So obvious and so simple in fact that I couldn't help wondering why on earth no-one had thought about it before.

That was what has now become the Voluntary Service Overseas cadet scheme and in spite of everything that has happened since, I still believe that for all round benefit this is, to me, the best part of the whole British Volunteer Programme. The surprise and delight at being wanted and being genuinely useful is far greater on leaving school than on leaving University.

With the entry of the Peace Corps and many other graduate recruiting organisations together with the very natural demand for qualified people, the graduate scheme has far outstripped the cadet scheme, and quite rightly. Graduates and qualified people, very naturally, can make a far more important contribution. As the whole scheme must be organised primarily for the people receiving help, the graduate scheme is far more important. Protest and destruction resulting from dissatisfaction and frusrtation is a sterile waste of energy and an escape from responsibility. Those who are really concerned with the fate of their fellow human beings, those who genuinely want to help improve and reform, and those who are bright enough to realise that constructive action is always better than destruction, cannot fail to find that work with the British Volunteer Programme is the most satisfying and rewarding experience of their lives.

This book is a fascinating account of the first ten exciting years of Voluntary Service Overseas. All of it is interesting but standing out like highlights in a dramatic picture are the stories and quotations supplied by the volunteers themselves. Not great prose perhaps, but the intensity of feeling, the pride and the pleasure through the simple words, and there suddenly, it's blindingly clear what Voluntary Service Overseas is all about.

Contents

Illustrations

11

Introduction

The volunteer movement is one of the strikingly hopeful phenomena of the postwar world – and it is a movement in which Britain gave the lead. It was in 1958 that Voluntary Service Overseas sent out its vanguard of eighteen volunteers. Ten years later there are more than 20,000 men and women from twenty countries serving in different parts of the developing world.

President Kennedy was quick to see the potentialities of this kind of cooperative venture and the American Peace Corps, which he founded, is now far and away the largest organisation in the field. Administered as a government agency and financed entirely out of US Government funds, the Peace Corps accounts for three-quarters of all the volunteers now serving abroad. In Canada, too, and in several European countries, the movement has expanded to a point where it deserves consideration as a substantial auxiliary in the world-wide battle against poverty and under-development.

A corollary of this expansion is the growing emphasis which the volunteer sending agencies now put on professionalism, both in the qualifications of those whom they recruit and in their approach to the tasks which they undertake. To some critics, preocupied perhaps by the opportunities open to the volunteers rather than by the needs of the developing countries, the change in emphasis is unwelcome; but there is no doubt that it reflects – and rightly – the concern of these countries to attack their problems at the roots and in the technically appropriate order. Nor can there be any rational argument against the proposition that those who send volunteers, if they wish to do more than demonstrate their goodwill, must send them to the jobs that most need doing – and see that they are technically equipped to do them. To achieve this, a professional approach is indispensable.

Voluntary Service Overseas, which pioneered this movement under the leadership of Alec Dickson,[1] started life as an agency recruiting only school-leavers. These were young men (and presently young women, too) who, by definition, lacked formal qualifications. In choosing them the selectors looked, certainly, for academic or other potential; but they looked especially for qualities of character, for an aptitude for leadership and a willingness to work for others, which would make them useful in a variety of situations. They were remarkably successful, and they were the trail-blazers for more than 2000 such 'cadet' volunteers from Britain who have since gone overseas, of whom some 400 are serving at this moment.

VSO's graduate division, formed in 1962 and quickly widened to include not only university graduates but those with all kinds of professional qualifications, has expanded fastest of all and now has close to a thousand volunteers in the field. In addition, three other agencies[2] cooperate with VSO inside the British Volunteer Programme and between them provide a further 250 to 300 volunteers. With the emphasis now on longer-term service, a growing proportion of these qualified volunteers now extend their service overseas for a second year. In all, including VSO's cadet division, the total for 1968–69 will be in the region of 1750 volunteers from Britain.

[1] Now Director of Community Service Volunteers, which does broadly similar work on the home front.
[2] These are: International Voluntary Service, United Nations Association, Catholic Institute for International Relations (see Chapter 5). Much of what is said in this book applies equally to them, but they are also engaged in other activities. This is primarily an account of the work of VSO, the only agency in Britain solely concerned with the recruitment, training and distribution of long-term volunteers.

More important than the simple expansion in numbers is the diversification of the work undertaken by volunteers. The largest proportion has always gone to teaching posts in the developing countries, some to universities and teacher training colleges but the majority to secondary schools, for everyone agrees that to expand their education programmes is the fundamental need for most developing countries. But with national development programmes now putting fresh emphasis on agriculture and forestry, or on industrial training, and with the general drive to expand medical and welfare services, the scope is constantly widening for the employment of volunteers in these fields. As the volunteer agencies try to meet these new demands, the proportion of volunteers employed in development work (as opposed to teaching) is steadily growing. The present emphasis is on finding the people with industrial, agricultural or medical qualifications of every kind, and at all levels.

The publicity given to the qualified volunteer has led some people to believe that there is no longer a place for the volunteer without higher qualifications. This is not so; but here, too, the trend is towards more development work and less teaching. There are plenty of opportunities for the boy from a farm institute or for the ex-apprentice who can undertake practical work or act as an instructor at a trade school. For straightforward teaching posts the competition is keen and the school-leaver is gradually being replaced by the holder of a university degree or the qualified teacher. The volunteer, whatever his or her qualifications, is essentially a stop-gap, whose function is it to hold the line until someone better qualified is available – and ultimately until the developing countries are able to meet their own needs for trained manpower. As standards of education rise in the developing world, and as more and more African and Asian pupils pass through newly established sixth forms and go on to universities, the opportunities for school-leaver volunteers are bound to diminish. The process is a slow one, for while some developing countries move out of the stage where they can use this kind of assistance, others are only now entering it. For these, the school-leaver with flexibility and enthusiasm to supplement his two or three 'A' levels is still a welcome reinforcement.

There is another context in which the school-leaver is a vital element in the whole picture of the volunteer movement. Among the new students entering our universities and colleges of education every year there is a sprinkling of these young men and women who already have behind them a year of voluntary service overseas. It is they, rather than any administrators or propagandists, who can spread the idea of such service and can give an accurate and contemporary account of its challenge and its rewards. They constitute the leaven in the lump, just as those who go out in steadily growing numbers from the universities and the colleges, from industry or agriculture or medicine, are able on their return to permeate our society with an awareness of the attitudes and the needs of the developing countries.

To build bridges of this kind is an important secondary function of the volunteer programme; in the long run it may turn out to have been the most important function of all. But the primary and immediate purpose must be to provide some of the skills which are so urgently needed in the under-privileged half of the world. To do this effectively calls for a constant process of reappraisal, to ensure that the services provided are of the right kind and are directed to where they will do most good. As the programme expands, and if it is to realise its full potential, it also calls for an ever-growing measure of public interest and support.

The question is not primarily one of fund-raising, although this is of course a constant preoccupation. Successive British governments have expressed their interest in the success of the programme by meeting approximately 75% of its cost – and they have been wise enough to do this without attempting to interfere with the voluntary character of the movement. (This still leaves a sizeable amount of money to be found from other sources: £170,000 for VSO in 1968.) More important is the attitude of mind of the public, and especially of employers, towards the whole idea of service in the developing countries. Many employers, both in industry and in the academic world, have enthusiastically embraced

16

the idea and have been liberal in releasing their employees or in deferring appointments so that young men and women could serve as volunteers. Very few of these, it is safe to say, have had reason to regret their decisions. Others, who remain cautious or sceptical, see perhaps less than the whole picture. Setting out with no thought of a material return, it is an exceptional volunteer who does not bring back a less tangible harvest in terms of experience, maturity of judgement and self-confidence. No employer is so rich in talent, nor is our society as a whole, that we can afford to underrate such benefits.

Chapter 1

Elizabethans, Old and New

Very early on a June morning, the coldest that any of them could remember, groups of campers were stirring under the trees of Hyde Park, shaking out their bedding, wrapping themselves in a variety of windcheaters and mufflers against the damp morning air. There was very little traffic, but even at that hour – for it was barely half past five – a swelling stream of pedestrians converging on central London. There was a sense of buoyancy in the air, an absence of restraint, most uncharacteristic of the British capital. People found themselves speaking to strangers and accepted the experience without distaste, even with exuberance. Along Piccadilly the newsvendors were shouting the odds and selling papers faster than they had done since VE day; and as their message became audible over the steady tramp of thousands of feet, the carefree mood of the crowd became even more pronounced. 'Everest Conquered', they were shouting – and at that moment in the dawn of Coronation Day, June 2nd, 1953, it seemed neither absurd nor vainglorious nor unreasonably romantic to feel a sudden thrill at the mere fact of being English.

Perhaps it is unwise to try at this distance to analyse that feeling. And yet, just because it was so soon to be dissipated and because it seems now so difficult to recapture, the effort may be worth while, if only to remind ourselves of attitudes of mind imperfectly masked by the sophistication of the nineteen-sixties. What was this 'new Elizabethan age', at whose birth the leader-writers told

18

us we were assisting and whose first triumphant symbol was a figure with an ice-axe on the roof of the world? What was the mainspring of that mood of jubilation? Was it pride, or patriotism, or nothing more than a hollow nostalgia for the 'dear, dead days beyond recall'?

Something, I would say, of all three – and, above all, an unusually frank avowal of that romantic instinct which the English find so difficult to recognise in themselves (in the Celtic fringe the vision is far clearer) but which underlies so much that is constant and vigorous in our history. Romantic, not in the modern Wardour Street sense, but in the older connotation which finds a common denominator in Francis Drake and Kipps and Lord Jim and T. E. Lawrence. Anything but exclusive, it may send one man in search of the Holy Grail, another after buried treasure, but always with a sense of opportunity and the will to grasp it. And there, I fancy, lies the clue. On that June morning the opportunities suddenly seemed limitless and if you had asked those damp figures in Piccadilly, so humdrum in their raincoats, where their ambitions lay, a surprising number of them would have replied in some mumbled paraphrase of Ulysses, who promised himself 'to strive, to seek, to find and not to yield'.

Of course it didn't last. How could it? How could an idea so fragile, a vision if you like, survive being tumbled against the realities of twentieth-century life, not only the hard facts of poverty and greed but the softer, more insidious temptations of security and the caution which the world misrepresents as good sense? It's no good urging a man to take the Golden Road to Samarkand, if you've brought him up to think of a semi-detached villa in Surbiton as his heart's desire.

There's no doubt that in the past things were easier in this sense. That first Elizabethan age, for instance, whose echoes so fired the adventurers of Fleet Street in 1953 – is it hopeless for us to try to recapture its simplicities, its proud certainties? Or, on another tack, is it wise? Now that there's no King of Spain with a beard to be singed, is there any point in trying to invent one? The mariners of old England, with whom those gallant leader-writers tried to identify themselves and us, were an inspiration, certainly; but were they altogether admirable as patterns of behaviour? Sir Francis Drake earned from his admiring compatriots the title of 'The Master Thief of the Unknown World', and of the generality of his followers H. A. L. Fisher has written:

'They were proud of England and their queen. They despised foreigners. They hated the Pope, the Turk, and the Devil, but perhaps most of all the Pope, who had allotted the East Indies to Portugal and the West Indies to Spain. Of international law, either as a need or as a fact, they had not the slightest suspicion. They regarded the high seas as a kind of no man's land upon which they might pillage and murder to their heart's content. Only to a few more curious spirits did marine enterprise suggest the possibility of missionary work.'

That last sentence introduces a new strand into a pattern of physical and spiritual expansion which was to become increasingly complex in the centuries that followed. Those high seas on which the Elizabethan buccaneers indulged their swash-buckling patriotism called their descendants to a variety of destinies. As soldiers, traders, missionaries, explorers, they pushed the horizons steadily back with a boldness that was unfailing and an unconscious assumption of superiority that now takes our breath away. The Atlantic, the Indian Ocean, the Pacific, in turn saw the little ships fanning out through the world; and in their wake there appeared on the fringes of the continents those tiny settlements from which, with gun or Bible or gold, the Englishman set out to remake the world.

Looking back now on that extraordinary sunburst of variegated endeavour, it is difficult to see behind it any single coherent motive force. Indeed, the attempt to find one leads us towards some embarrassing conclusions. That antipathy for foreigners, which Fisher noted, was certainly a powerful incentive in the early days; and as time passed and our forebears grew more sure of themselves, this was merely transmuted into a conviction, sometimes patronising, often arrogant, that fate had somehow singled out the British as rightful masters of the world. Benevolent masters, of course; disinterested and paternal, ready to unfold to the less enlightened those mysteries of sound government and high moral purpose which had been vouchsafed to them in an exclusive revelation. That revelation the British were determined to share, indeed they felt morally bound to share it, with the lesser breeds without the law. The effort might be painful and (what was worse) costly, but it had to be made. For the plain fact was, as the British saw it, that they, the British, were right.

To those on the receiving end, the picture of course looked very different. Here and there, sometimes with dismay but more often with astonishment, the British were made aware of the fact that others did not share their own view of themselves or of their world mission. An English traveller in the Sudan at the end of the eighteenth century, after a meeting with the Muslim ruler of Darfur, noted that this distant potentate regarded the English, along with other Europeans, as belonging to 'a small tribe, cut off by the singularity of colour and features, and still more by their impiety, from the rest of mankind'.[1] It was easy to dismiss this kind of reaction as eccentric, and others were more favourably impressed than the ruler of Darfur by the self-confident bearing of the British. Occasionally they went further, kissing with genuine enthusiasm the rod which the British laid on their backs. More often they were resentful, obstinate in their defence of habits, beliefs, dominions, which they had no wish to abandon. Then it became necessary to coerce them and to this task, too, the British proved themselves equal. It was unfortunate, of course. It would have been much more satisfactory to communicate the benefits of civilisation through persuasion and the simple force of high example – but where these failed, the British did not shrink from the harsh duty to enforce the pattern of a social and moral order of whose superiority they had no doubts.

This was the genesis of imperialism, which has been well described as 'an overflow of energy which Africa and Asia

[1] W. G. Browne, *Travels in Africa, Egypt and Syria 1792–8*, quoted by Norman Daniel in *Islam, Europe & Empire*.

absorbed'.[1] For better and for worse it conditioned the world in which we live today; and in many of our present attitudes towards the world and its problems we are consciously or unconsciously following through, or reacting against, the attitudes of our grandfathers in the high noon of British imperialism, during the latter part of the reign of Queen Victoria.

Since 1945, with the imperial territories jostling each other into the promised land of independence, the concept of imperialism has been on the defensive. Yet it would be as foolish now to belittle its achievements as to disguise its shortcomings. It provided scope for the exercise of humane and intelligent authority on the most exalted plane. It also afforded an opportunity for commercial skulduggery of the lowest kind. Its motives, in fact, were bewilderingly mixed and its least attractive characteristic was a certain complacency, an unwavering assumption of self-righteousness and moral superiority. While this might sometimes be justified, it also provided a screen behind which the unscrupulous and the merely lazy disguised their failure to live up to the standards set by the best of their countrymen. It was used too, or misused, to justify what many of us today would point to as the central weakness of the imperial approach: its failure to establish a workable relationship between the governors and the governed in so many of the territories for which Britain assumed responsibility and whose destinies she controlled.

This weakness was inherent in the nature of the system. To govern well, to exercise authority over others, whether it be within a firm, a country or an empire, the governor must feel in himself a superiority which qualifies him for the exercise of his authority. He must not merely claim, but be certain, that he possesses a higher degree of knowledge, a surer sense of values, a wider experience and a more highly developed instinct for appropriate action than those whose destinies he is called upon to direct. And the inevitable corollary is that he will see in these dependants the reverse of what he sees in himself. He will be conscious (and the more seriously he takes his responsibilities, the more conscious

[1] Daniel, op. cit.

will he be) of their frailty and their inexperience. He will feel for them the protective instinct of a true parent – and, like many otherwise excellent parents, he may find it very hard to recognise the moment when his protection is no longer necessary or when the true interests of the child demand that it be encouraged to stand on its own feet. In the case of the British imperialists of the nineteenth century, the best of whom were men with a profound sense of moral purpose and an impregnable integrity, it was natural to adopt towards the subject peoples of the empire an attitude of detachment which was essentially paternal. By virtue of their education and training, in terms of the technical and material resources of the government which they represented, and above all because of the power they exercised, they were seen by others and could hardly be blamed if they saw themselves as gods, able to change and direct as completely, if less arbitrarily, as Poseidon or Pallas Athene the fortunes of the subject populations about them.

More important for our immediate purpose than the spirit which animated the imperial age is the extraordinary range of opportunities which that age offered to the enterprising Englishman. And in this sense the imperial age persisted until the outbreak of Hitler's war; as late as 1938 the map of the world, with those uncompromising swathes of red splashed across the continents, beckoned him to choose any of a dozen promising destinies. Merely to be English was to have a head start on the world; to possess in addition the connections and qualifications which, by and large, were still available only to a privileged minority, was to hold a passport to distinction. From the sub-continent of India to the smallest island dependency in the West Indies, there was a constant and reassuring demand for British administrators, judges, clergymen, clerks, police officers and all the assorted instruments of colonial rule. For the more sought-after posts the gateway of opportunity was indeed narrow, but Britain's maritime supremacy and the development of overseas trade offered glittering prizes to the enterprising young man who lacked the 'right background' for positions of political influence; while, if it was a concern for the welfare of his fellow man rather than the profit motive that animated him, the mission field was world-wide and wide open, from West Africa to the coast of China. No one with ambition, a sense of purpose or a simple taste for adventure could fail to find, somewhere on that imperial globe, an outlet for his energies or a chance to make his fortune. As an old man put it to me the other day, recalling with nostalgia the wide horizons of his youth: 'Wherever you looked, north, south, east or west, there was just Us – it was marvellous!'

There is a reflection of this in the literature of the early part of this century, and especially in the books written for boys. How could any boy brought up on Kipling and Henty, on Beau Geste and Greenmantle and the Four Feathers, resist the siren song of adventure? How could he not feel that the world was waiting for him to set his stamp upon it? And if somehow he grew to manhood without falling victim to these, there still lay in wait for him Conrad and C. E. Montague, *Blackwood's Magazine*, Flecker and Chesterton and a dozen more who flew the flag of romance without diffidence or apology. The wonder is that any young Englishman remained at home in this island after the age of twenty.

This element of romance, or pure adventure, was surely an important one in the development of imperialism. At twenty a young man may not have, or know that he has – or be able to persuade others that he has – the qualities that will one day make him governor of a province. Such a destiny, could he envisage it, might well alarm or repel him. He is much more likely to be thinking, as he embarks on the first step of a career, not of its conclusion (which at that moment seems infinitely distant and incalculable) but of the present and the immediate future: of what fun it will be to escape from the confines of the familiar and to launch out on the open sea of life. So it must have been with many of those who in later life found themselves wielding the responsibilities of empire; the initial impetus must often have been a simple desire for adventure, to which was added, as time passed and maturity developed a sense of responsibility and an awareness of particular gifts, the ambition to achieve this or that goal, leave this or that individual mark in the margin of history.

Chapter 2

Postwar Attitudes

Between 1939 and 1945, a brief moment in the calendar of eternity, the pattern of the world was changed. The old order, so full of promise and imperfection, had endured with little outward modification from the middle of the nineteenth century until 1914 and had survived even that shock to enjoy the Indian summer which ended in 1939. In 1945 it stood suddenly condemned, like an ancestral home whose bewildered heir found himself all at once unequal to the task of maintaining it.

It was a traumatic moment for Britain, involving as it did the renunciation of a role in the world which had become second nature. It brought in its train all kinds of adjustments, both material and psychological, which were anything but easy to a people accustomed to claim for themselves (though without thinking very much about it) a certain primacy in the counsels of the world. It was made, of course, still more difficult by our domestic preoccupations, by the hectic aftermath of war, by the sudden realisation that whatever was to be done about our position in the world there were all sorts of repairs and renovations which urgently needed to be undertaken in the structure of our own social life. It was as though, just when we were rolling up our sleeves to tackle the plumbing, we had been told that there was dry rot in the main beams supporting the roof.

The emergency – for such it undoubtedly was – took different people in different ways. Resignation rubbed shoulders with a defiant refusal to accept the facts of the situation. There were those who argued equably that we should forget our old pretensions and accept the modest status of another Holland or Denmark, while to others the merest suggestion of withdrawal from any of the responsibilities of empire was the signal for apoplectic protest. Effectively, the issue was settled with merciful promptness when the postwar government decided to grant independence to India. Once the crown had lost its brightest jewel, there was little point in being possessive about the lesser stones. All the same the years from 1947 onwards, during which we watched, with a mixture of pride and resentment, the rapid shrinking of the empire, were difficult years; more difficult perhaps than they need have been because we found it hard to appreciate just what had happened, and was still happening, in the world about us.

The central fact was easy enough to grasp: that the war had so weakened traditional attitudes that authority everywhere was undermined. The trade unionist challenged the boss, youth challenged age; even the church and the monarchy no longer appeared sacrosanct; and in the mêlée every sort of underdog suddenly astonished himself and those who thought themselves his superiors by barking most insistently in pursuit of rights, privileges, possessions, all the fruits of life which under the old order had been labelled 'forbidden'. It was confusing in the extreme, not least to some of the underdogs who had no experience of barking and were not really sure they wanted to bark at all; and of course it was infinitely disturbing to those who found themselves barked at and who took little comfort from telling each other that there was no knowing where it would all end.

Beyond this general shifting of accepted values and priorities there were, I think, three more specific factors which encouraged a reappraisal on all sides of the prevailing pattern of international relationships. There was, to begin with, the vast humiliation which the West had suffered at the hands of the East. The Japanese conquest of Malaya, Burma and the Pacific islands had exploded the myth of white supremacy. Henceforth it would be impractical, as well as impudent, to sermonise about the equality of man and

26

at the same time forbid Indians to walk on the Mall in Simla or Egyptians to join the Gezira Club in Cairo. In this sphere too, every dog felt the inclination to have his day and it seemed suddenly very difficult to deny him.

Then there was the shock that Europe had given itself and the shuddering recollection of the abyss out of which it had just – and with heartbreaking difficulty – managed to emerge. The destruction of the cities of Europe, the virtual breakdown of civilised existence in large tracts of the continent, the savagery of the gas-chambers, the endless and horrifying catalogue of inhumanity and the trail it left across Europe of refugees, orphans, physical and mental cripples – all this brought home, even to the phlegmatic English, who had escaped direct experience of the innermost hell of degradation, what it must mean to be the victim of hunger, injustice, tyranny, brutality. It gave them a glancing acquaintance with these evils and so a faint and fleeting sense of kinship with those for whom they were a part of daily experience. I remember a prisoner-of-war whom I met in the spring of 1945. He had just been marched by his captors from one end of Germany to the other; his boots were burst, his beard was unkempt and for a month he had been living on rotten potatoes. I gave him a razor blade and a pair of bootlaces, and apologised for the fact that I had nothing more to offer. His eyes peered at me out of deep hollows and his beard stirred in what I realised was a smile. 'It's amazing how well you can get along on nothing,' he said, 'if that's all you've got.' It was a lesson hard-learned, but humanising.

Finally there was a factor which did not make itself felt at once but which gathered strength in the postwar period, perhaps as a reaction against the inclination of those in authority to tackle new problems in old ways, and consequently to make little headway in solving the dilemmas of an uneasy world. This was the general upsurge of youth everywhere, rebellious, critical, irreverent, self-confident, impatient of the old nostrums and of those who peddled them, impatient above all of what it saw as the double-talk, and double-dealing, too, of the older generations on a whole series of subjects from politics to fashion. In Britain as in the world at

27

large, this emphasis on the importance of youth, its right to be consulted, its claim to have a hand in things, was a genuinely new element in the human equation. It was invigorating, with its assumption that every Gordian knot could be sliced through; it was alarming, with its contemptuous dismissal of the world's most revered preconceptions, its refusal to acknowledge frontiers, whether on the map or in the mind. And its potential was enormous, if only it could hit on the right pattern of organisation.

But this was precisely what was lacking. In those first postwar years, with all the horrid and exhilarating urgency gone out of our lives, youth asked for a lead and age was too weary to give it. As a nation we were the victims of a tremendous anticlimax. So long accustomed to concentrating all our energies on one immediately recognisable target, it was disheartening, just when we felt inclined to lie back on beds of amaranth and moly, to find ourselves faced by other tasks, less clear-cut, less dramatic and heroic, but not, it rapidly became clear, any easier. Like the lotus-eaters we felt

> '*Is there confusion in the little isle?*
> *Let what is broken so remain.*
> *The Gods are hard to reconcile:*
> *'Tis hard to settle order once again.*
> *There is confusion worse than death,*
> *Trouble on trouble, pain on pain,*
> *Long labour unto aged breath,*
> *Sore task to hearts worn out with*
>   *many wars*
> *And eyes grown dim with gazing on the*
>   *pilot-stars.*'

This mood of disenchantment, natural enough in the circumstances, was worse than useless to the young for whom the end of the way implied frustration as well as release. Screwed up like their elders to meet a challenge, ready like them to break a lance in defence of aims so familiar as no longer to need definition, the young found themselves abruptly stranded on the threshold of an empty battlefield. Their weapons untried, and all their reserves of hopeful energy undimmed by prosaic experience, they were stripped for action – but denied a goal. They found themselves excluded from the work of reconstruction, to which their elders turned with resignation, and consigned instead to the empty routine of conscription, manning without enthusiasm the battlements whose guns had been silenced and performing with understandable distaste the duties of an army of occupation in the blackened ruins of Hitler's Germany.

The decade after 1945 then was a difficult one for all of us, and most of all, perhaps, for the young, those who felt that they had missed something and who looked for a means of fulfilment and found none. It was in any case a dreary time in which to be young, a grey world of ration books and bomb sites when petrol was short and trains ran late, a utility world in which the best of everything seemed to be second best and the rest far worse. We all of us grew impatient at its restrictions and expressed our dissatisfaction in whatever way came most naturally to us, heckling the politicians, writing letters to *The Times*, emigrating to Australia or simply 'knocking the establishment' in a characteristic phrase of the period. Kingsley Amis produced, in 'Lucky Jim', an appropriate anti-hero for the times, and Bernard Levin set himself up as a youthful Socrates, an impudent gadfly on the flank of society.

The malaise, of course, went far deeper than a sense of discontent at the prevailing inefficiency. For there was a growing consciousness of national ineptitude, of our inadequacy to the tasks facing us at home quite apart from the responsibilities which were still ours in the rest of the world. Other countries seemed to be recovering far more easily from the devastation of the war; and it was with a bitter reluctance that we were forced to acknowledge the extent to which our own recovery was dependent on the help of the Americans. We longed to reassert our independence but our reactions seemed to have grown slow, our national muscles felt flabby. We leaned too much for reassurance on the memory of Dunkirk and the Battle of Britain, and at the same time we

29

became uneasily aware that foreigners, some with sympathy and others with malice, were writing us off as a nation of has-beens.

It was from this mood of disillusionment and self-criticism that we hoped to escape in the enthusiasm of 1953, when all the ancient grandeur of the coronation ceremony and the proud echoes of the word 'Elizabethan' stirred us to what felt like a reawakening. The picture of a young queen, whose loyal chief minister was the very embodiment of the nation's strength, gave us the welcome sense that even though

> '*We are not now that strength which in old days*
> *Moved earth and heaven; that which we are, we are;*
> *One equal temper of heroic hearts,*
> *Made weak by time and fate, but strong in will . . .*'

And the figure with the ice-axe on the top of Everest seemed to prove it.

Alas, something went wrong. Perhaps it was that there was too strong an element of propaganda about it all, too deliberate a promotion campaign with too little of the genuine will for a renewal behind it. At all events, the enthusiasm evaporated, the skies which had seemed to clear clouded over again and we found ourselves back once more in the petty round of material preoccupation from which we had thought to escape. Abroad, we found ourselves constantly, and reluctantly, on the retreat, and when we tried – perhaps with some distorted idea in our minds of that need for renewal – to show ourselves 'strong in will', the attempt ended in the shabby deceptions of Suez, when the British appeared to the world as anything but 'one equal temper of heroic hearts'. The episode seemed to confirm that we had lost our touch, and it signalled an important stage in the decline of our influence in the world.

Suez was a reminder too of an important, indeed an inescapable, fact about the postwar world. It was *one* world, in a way that it had never been before. For all its apparent impotence, the United Nations was a more influential organisation than the old League of Nations had ever been and it was far harder now for a nation bent on going it alone to have its way against the opposition of the rest of the world community.

Apart from anything else, we all knew much more about each other. The tremendous and rapid improvement in communications, especially the development of radio and television, made the world instantly aware of what was happening – or what some skilful publicist wanted the world to believe was happening – in the remoter corners of the globe. To a large extent this was the result of international rivalry and suspicion. The iron curtain was still a thing of stark reality, but its very existence prompted those on each side of it to go to great lengths to discover what was going on on the other side, if only in order to make political capital out of it. But there was sympathy as well as hostility behind this probing, as least as far as the general public was concerned. There was a sense that the world had a common interest in finding solutions to the problems which were common to mankind – and this stirring of a sense of world citizenship was made more urgent by the fearful knowledge that the penalties of failure were greater than they had ever been. With uneasy fascination the world watched the race between the two giants of the eastern and the western worlds for supremacy in the field of atomic warfare.

There was also a more fruitful aspect to this closer interest which the nations now took in the affairs of their neighbours. The problems which the war had left behind were of such dimensions that self-help could no longer deal with them; the habit of international cooperation grew out of the prostration of so much of the civilised world. In rebuilding Europe, the United States showed an energetic concern which won the Americans few friends, but which achieved in a surprisingly short space of time an astonishing success. From Europe, spurred on by the desire to compete with the Russians for the loyalties of half the world, but animated too by a noble vision of the world as it might be and an outlook not unlike the old British imperial outlook, with its mercantile and its humanitarian aspects, the Americans directed their energies farther afield. The pattern of organisation provided by the Marshall Plan was adapted, some of the instruments of

European recovery – in particular the World Bank – were re-directed, to attempt something that had never been attempted in the world before. The objective was the third of those Four Freedoms which President Roosevelt had postulated as the allied aims in the war: Freedom from Want. The idea – and it seems almost inconceivable now that it could have been a novel one less than twenty years ago – was to put a floor under poverty everywhere, to establish certain basic minima of food, housing, clothing and health below which no nation need sink or should be allowed to sink. It was an idea as grandiose as any that history has known, a challenge to the imagination as well as to the productive and administrative skills of the leaders of the free world.

Again it was the Americans who took the lead, but this was not, of course, an exclusively American initiative. In the nineteen-fifties, while India had attained independence and other territories of the old British empire were struggling towards it, Whitehall still held responsibility for a string of dependencies at various stages of development. To their advancement, material as well as political, Britain made what contribution she could in her strai-tened circumstances; and when they in their turn ran up in place of the Union Jack their own new flags and assumed control of their own destinies, they were given a modest start in life in the way of grants or loans from the British Treasury, while some of the former colonial servants stayed on to serve their new masters. But Britain's resources in the postwar world were too modest, her own economic situation too parlous, for her to play a major part in solving the problems of others; and at the same time it happened that the vagaries of international trade turned against these new-comers to the comity of nations. Dependent for their living, as most of them were, on the scale of primary products like sugar, cocoa, rubber and jute, they saw the prices of these goods falling all through the 'fifties, while the price of manufactured goods – the very things they needed if they were to realise their dreams of modernisation and development – rose with the same regularity, leaving the new nations fighting what seemed an endless losing battle for solvency. Political independence, they came to realise,

1. (*above left*) Mr. Alec Dickson,
C.B.E., originator of Voluntary
Service Overseas and now
Director of Community Service
Volunteers

2. (*above*) Director of VSO, Mr.
D. H. Whiting, O.B.E., addressing
volunteers at a briefing course

3. A volunteer from a Farm
Institute working in Zambia

4
Sierra Leone: measuring mangrove roots and calculating the number of oysters growing

5
Uganda: teaching blind children to read braille

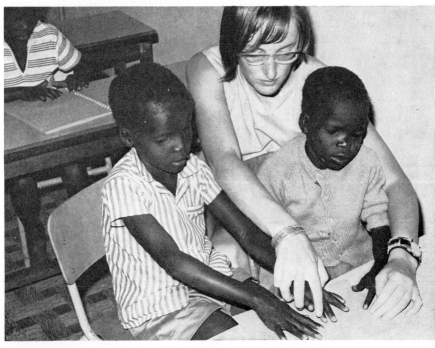

was only half the battle – and generally the easier half. The real slog came when they tried to establish a stable economic foundation.

These hard lessons in the realities of nationhood, coupled with the growth of a sense of world responsibility, encouraged the leaders of both the new nations and the old to take a fresh look at the way in which their mutual relationship was organised. Under the old dispensation it had appeared preordained that the advanced industrial countries of Europe and North America should produce manufactured goods and sell them to what were coming to be thought of as the 'under-developed countries' (a term presently to be replaced by the more tactful euphemism 'developing countries'), in return for the raw materials and the cash crops which were all that these more primitive societies were geared to produce. Such a scheme of things appeared logical and orderly, especially to those who could themselves expect to reap the rewards of industrial expansion in a steadily growing world market. But as the new men of Asia and Africa emancipated themselves, went to Oxford or the London School of Economics, served their terms in gaol or on the Seychelles and then became the first prime ministers of these emergent states – why, then the pattern suddenly seemed far less satisfactory. With impatience, and often with far from adequate preparation, they set about changing it. And, of course, they wanted to do everything at once, to make overnight the great leap forward which would bring them not merely solvency, but wealth, prestige, the estimation of a world in which at last they would be the equals of anyone. From the establishment of a cement factory it was only a short step to the creation of a national textile industry; from there to a steel mill, and before long to the formation of a national airline – for which, of course, only the most up-to-date and sophisticated aircraft in the world were considered suitable.

It was easy for the rest of us to smile at their mistakes and to shake our heads over the predictable muddles that ensued. It was less easy to acknowledge the extent to which we shared the responsibility for them or to make up our minds to do what we

C 33

could to help to put them right. And muddles there often were, in the first heady stages of self-government, when enthusiasm outran discretion. Slowly and painfully it came to be realised that to stand on its own feet a nation needed more than mere will-power and material resources. If it was to make the most of both, it still needed the money to exploit them and the advice of those versed in the complications of modern life. It needed – and inevitably these new nations lacked – the experience of men trained in a more complex society, equipped to view a particular project in the wider perspective of national development, and to ensure, not merely that it was viable in economic terms, but that it harmonised with the larger needs of that particular country at that particular stage in its evolution.

Out of all this grew a whole series of new organisations, both national and international, whose aim it was to provide the necessary framework of experience and expertise – as well as the money – to enable the new nations to make the most of their potential. At first, in the thick of the cold war, these efforts were seldom disinterested. In competition with each other, the larger powers were out to win friends and influence people, and aid was often just another weapon in their armoury.

This was not necessarily a bad thing, since whatever the motives behind it the aid was forthcoming, and rivalry between the givers provided for the recipients the chance to do some shrewd bargaining. Some odd situations resulted and a few of the most loyal supporters of this or that world camp were upset to find that their loyalty brought them a meagre return, while the more obdurate neutralists like President Nasser reaped a rich reward. However, the habit of providing aid became established and there was something to be said for being frank about it and realising that both sides had something to gain from the bargain. For this was a fact that needed to be established. The component parts of this most unequally constituted world were coming to realise that they were interdependent. If one country needed machines, another needed markets. If this meant giving away a few machines at first in order to be able to sell more later, there was a sound mercantile basis for providing aid – quite apart from any human-itarian justification it might have.

This was one conclusion that emerged from the early aid pro-grammes set up in the nineteen-fifties. Another, more depressing one, was that aid, in whatever spirit it was given, provided a developing country with no automatic passport to progress and plenty. The machines might come, and the experts to maintain and explain them; a whole pattern of interrelated activities might be organised in such a way as to make the most fruitful use of the equipment and the technical assistance which had been pro-vided. But the problem remained of fitting this whole pattern into the existing economic and social framework of the developing country – and here the planners and the experts came up against a formidable obstacle in the shortage of trained manpower in the whole of the developing world. You can take a shepherd or an agricultural labourer and train him to mind a machine; but where, in a population in which shepherds and agricultural labourers predominate, do you find the foremen, the supervisors, the managers who can carry the whole process forward and eventually take it over as a going national concern when the foreign experts withdraw? As the scale of the world's problems revealed them-selves, as more and more developing countries began to call on the experience of those who had solved these specific economic problems elsewhere, it became apparent that the solutions they proposed depended for their success on the existence of a kind of human infrastructure which was almost invariably lacking in terri-tories long accustomed to a dependent status. It could be created, but not overnight – and to create it at all required not only instructors at all levels, but the existence of a sufficient number of trainees who must themselves have enough education to be able to understand and absorb instruction in technical and managerial skills.

A shortage of such people might make itself felt in a dozen ways. It was illustrated by unused machinery which rusted in the harbours where it had been dumped as 'aid' or remained in its crates for lack of anyone competent to unpack and assemble it.

It was more subtly illustrated by the creation of sizeable industries in countries which possessed no substantial outlets for the goods produced. It was most forcefully illustrated by political failures on the part of governments, which set in motion elaborate plans for development and then saw them wither for lack of proper coordination between government departments often only a few hundred yards apart – but each lacking the trained manpower at a secondary level to ensure such coordination. The problem was one of education in its widest sense, of the lack of that infrastructure of trained people who could understand a blue-print and make it work.

In these emergent countries then, there was a serious, often a desperate, need for all the levers of development, for the money and the machines which would transform life. These could only come from the technologically advanced societies of North America and Europe. But even where they were forthcoming, the most ambitious efforts to make use of them were often frustrated by this human bottleneck, which reduced the eager current of hopes to a sad, slow trickle of performance. It was inexpressibly tantalising. To be held up here, on the threshold of what has been called the revolution of rising expectations, by a stumbling-block so mundane yet so insuperable – it was like boarding an aircraft in the confident assumption of a swift and easy journey, only to be turned out again into the unhappy limbo of the departure lounge because some minor but indispensable component refused to function.

Meanwhile, in the advanced countries, as we have seen, circumstances had combined to induce a willingness to help and to create the machinery for providing material and technical assistance to the countries which needed it. The motives for doing so were mixed, with elements of political gamesmanship and commercial enterprise working alongside the new liberal internationalism of the postwar period. Individually or in concert through the various agencies of the United Nations, the old world was learning to accept its responsibilities in the new. Studies were made, experts recruited, programmes launched. In his inaugural address in 1949

President Truman announced, under the famous 'Point Four' (a landmark in the history of development aid) a 'bold new programme' of technical assistance to the under-developed world. In the following year the British Government took the lead in launching the Colombo Plan, a joint programme by the members of the Commonwealth for 'Co-operative Economic Development in South and South-east Asia'. In the years that followed similar programmes were set on foot, with similar objectives, to meet the needs of every part of the under-developed world, until their initials formed a bewildering catalogue of international good intentions.

The disappointing thing was to see how few of these intentions came to anything. Or rather – for they did find expression in any number of steel mills and oil refineries and chemical plants and all the other unappetising fruits of progress – to observe how small a dent the planners were able to make on the central problem which they were called upon to solve. For the gulf which separated the old world from the new, the developed from the developing, the rich (to be blunt) from the poor, obstinately refused to be bridged. Indeed, despite all the efforts of these world engineers, it was the rich who grew richer, not the poor, and the gulf between them steadily and remorselessly widened.

More cause here for disenchantment, more ammunition for those who disliked the whole idea of overseas aid, asking querulously (from their comfortable vantage-point) why other nations should not pull themselves up by their own bootstraps as we had done, more discouragement for those already tired of 'ever climbing up the climbing wave'. And if this was the effect on the older generation, on the politicians and the planners and the 'experts' who were trying to find solutions to these novel and disconcerting problems, what of the young, those who had not been called upon to share in their efforts and were only witnesses of their apparent unsuccess? For them, if they thought about it at all, there semed here to be fresh evidence of the inadequacy of the old guard to their new responsibilities. It was easy for youth to conclude that age would make a mess of things again, as it had done before, and that all the fine talk of a new Elizabethan age was so much old flummery designed to disguise the fact that things were to go on much as they had always done.

Not that anyone took much notice yet of what the young thought. Indeed, it was a novel and to most people a distasteful idea, in the early 'fifties, that youth, as such, had a point of view – or any right to one. Much more general was the tendency to think the postwar generation just another problem, a particularly tiresome and intractable one. 'No values', people said, 'no sense of responsibility' – which was just another way of saying that the young rejected the fixed points in the horizon of their elders, as youth had always done, and made no bones about saying so, which was something new and disturbing. And the more the older generations showed that they were disturbed by it, the more youth played them up, edging towards the frontiers of anarchy with a restless impudence which was self-conscious but unplanned, vigorous but at the same time aimless, so that its manifestations were seldom constructive and generally – as they were designed to be – offensive.

This was a natural, perhaps even an inevitable, part of the disruption of that old pattern of society which collapsed with the war. The temptation was for society to attempt to reassert itself, to bang the table and insist on the observance of codes which had served well in the past. But it was inherent in the postwar malaise that the authority to insist was no longer there, or no longer acknowledged at any rate; and like a schoolmaster who has lost his authority, the more society tried to regain control, alternating between the use of the stick and of the carrot, the more the errant pupil realised the strength of his position and took advantage of it. The fact was that, like so many other things in the postwar world, neither the sticks nor the carrots which society had at its disposal were any longer as effective as they had been in the old days. In the way of sticks, well, there was conscription of course, serving less and less purpose but still regarded as a useful way of 'knocking some of the nonsense out of them' and seeing that they had their hair cut regularly; but it was distressingly easy for a sharp lad to find his way to a cushy billet in the army and do as much harm

38

as he could outside – and at the public's expense, too. As for carrots, just what was there to offer to an enterprising youngster in a country which the world agreed had shot its bolt, and with the empire disintegrating into a jumble of states with unpronounceable names and a built-in suspicion of the motives of all Englishmen, young or old? Where was he to look for adventure in a world in which 'the Rudyards cease from Kipling and the Haggards ride no more'? Lord Jim was out and all thought of magic casements; from now on it was Lucky Jim who looked out on the world through the rainswept windows of his bedsitter.

It was only later that society, having at last given up the quest for its vanished authority – having indeed submitted, with an ill grace, to something very like domination by this younger generation – discovered that behind the restless and untidy façade which youth presented to the world there were some unsuspected elements. It is difficult now to say just when these made themselves apparent, and of course they were always there to the discerning eye. The mood of that Coronation Day crowd showed it, and even before that, in all the squalid muddle of Europe in the aftermath of the war, there had been islands of something better and more hopeful in the work camps and refugee centres in which young people from this country worked for and alongside the human debris of Hitler's Europe. But it was easy to overlook these or to dismiss them as the work of cranks and as exceptions to the general rule. The majority, in the jargon of the day, 'couldn't care less' and made a point of it.

If one had to isolate the turning-point, I should plump for the autumn of 1956 when a bewildered and resentful British expeditionary force was immobilised in Port Said. That in itself prompted a lot of angry heart-searching – but what was more important, in the context which we are considering, was a very different kind of expeditionary force, much more hurriedly and less efficiently organised (indeed scarcely organised at all, in the sense of having any established pattern or hierarchy or discipline) which headed at much the same time for a European destination. Russian tanks were in Budapest, and along the Austrian side of the Hungarian border appeared, in that glum October of 1956, a haphazard collection of camps and caravans whose occupants, all beards and duffle-coats, set themselves to salvage work. It was lives they were salvaging, as the refugees staggered across the border into their arms; and the essential point is that no one sent them there, no one 'coordinated' their activities, there were no questions asked in the Security Council about what they were doing (and no lies told in reply). They didn't do it for national prestige, or to win export markets or even out of a conscious desire to live up to what they would have thought it pretentious to call a tradition. They were young and they went simply because they thought it worth while, even necessary, in much the same spirit as the bank clerks and factory workers who went off as volunteers to fight the Kaiser in 1914; and it's no disrespect to them or to the bank clerks and factory workers to say that, apart from anything else, to go seemed more adventurous than to stay at home. At last the myth of the new Elizabethan age was taking on some substance.

I call this the turning point because here was the first really noticeable expression of an impulse which must have been gathering strength in silence. It was a spontaneous expression, called forth by a particular set of circumstances – but the impulse was more generalised, like the mood of discontent which chance may turn into a revolution. It was a foretaste of things to come, an indication of resources untapped, and it had a bearing on the story I have to tell.

Chapter 3

The Birth of an Idea

Among those who turned up on the Hungarian border in that winter of 1956–57 was one man considerably older than most of those around him, for whom the experience had a particular significance. This was Alec Dickson, a man of unusual energy and originality of mind, whose background – that of an unorthodox, not to say rebellious, civil servant in the twilight of the colonial era – set him a little apart from the young idealists of this untidy crusade. For them, the episode provided a first encounter with some of the uglier facts of twentieth-century life. Escaping, for the first time in their lives, from the strait-jacket of the welfare state, they had an opportunity here to exercise muscles developed but still untried. For him it was more a chance to test in practice a theory as yet imperfectly formulated. Looking back on the experience long afterwards, he found that his most vivid recollection was 'not of the refugees, but of young students from Britain finding satisfaction in being used'. He saw that in this unlooked-for emergency there was a sense of fulfilment for individuals who found themselves valued and depended upon – and for whom life at home offered no comparable opportunity. The idea strengthened a conviction already shaping itself in his mind.

As a government servant in Nigeria, Dickson had often chafed at the restraints of official life. But while his relations with his superiors had not always been easy, he had a particular aptitude for working with those younger than himself and it was in this context that he had come to concentrate his efforts. He had helped to organise in Nigeria the Man o'War Bay centre, which provided for young Nigerians a training in citizenship and leadership; and 1956 found him, with the same sort of ideas in mind, leading a UNESCO technical assistance mission in Iraq. The aim was to try to involve the young in the development of their own social environment, to encourage in them a sense of responsibility and to awaken them to the realisation that in the modern world where their countrymen were claiming independence it was they, the rising generation, who must learn to stand on their own feet and galvanise their own society into activity.

In Iraq it proved uphill work. Dickson was oppressed by the thought that instead of young Iraqis it was middle-aged foreigners like himself who were providing the motive force. When the mission ended its task and he returned to England – an England where youth was constantly being lectured for its aimlessness and irresponsibility – Dickson found himself brooding over the reasons for his own sense of dissatisfaction. What was wrong with life, whether in Iraq or in England, that it seemed to offer so little to fire the imagination of the younger generation? What was the central weakness in a pattern of social organisation which provided no recognised function for youth and did nothing to help youth to realise its potential?

The problem, as Dickson saw it, was two-fold. First it was necessary to find some way of persuading young citizens anywhere that the community needed them, that indeed there were areas in which they could help the community in a way that middle-aged 'experts' could not. Second, there was need for a stimulus, a challenge, which could restore to life some of the excitement it had held for previous generations and which seemed to have been squeezed out of it by the benevolent machinery of the welfare state.

Looking back now, these ideas seem straightforward enough; in 1956 they were revolutionary – and precisely at this stage in the evolution of his thoughts came that episode on the Hungarian border. Untidy and inconclusive, it provided the missing link of practical experience. It showed that when the challenge presented itself, the response was forthcoming. It gave some indication of the human resources which were going to waste for lack of an objective. It convinced Dickson that with energy and imagination it must be possible to use those resources and to direct them to strengthening some of the weak points in the structure of twentieth-century society.

The initial difficulty was to persuade society itself of the need for an initiative on the lines which he envisaged. Officialdom in Britain was unenthusiastic, was indeed highly sceptical of the contribution which youth might make to resolving the problems of the world. It was not just that the postwar generation seemed to its elders more than usually perverse and uncooperative, though that was an important factor. More important still was the widespread sense, in a world faced with new and bewildering problems of economic and social development, that the answers could only be provided by the technically proficient. It was the age of the expert, and it seemed eccentric to look for salvation to the young and inexperienced. Moreover to suggest, as Dickson began to do in the unwelcoming corridors of the Colonial and Commonwealth Relations Offices, that Britain should not merely recruit inexperienced young Englishmen to help with these problems, but should contemplate sending them out into the under-developed world, ran doubly counter to the prevailing winds in Whitehall. The trend – and the Suez fiasco had greatly strengthened it – was to extricate ourselves from foreign commitments which seemed to promise only pain and humiliation. To propose that we should undertake fresh ones, and in a spirit of deliberate amateurism at that, was plainly laughable.

Laughable it might be, and eccentric – but Dickson was not alone in his approach to the question. His own ideas were still tentative, though they were shaking down into a recognisable and coherent pattern, when there appeared in *The Spectator* in February 1957 an article which reinforced his thinking and focused it on a more precise objective. The article was by George Edinger, who had worked as a journalist in Singapore and whose experience as a trade union official collaborating closely with his Asian colleagues had led him to see things in a different light from the usual run of expatriates in a British colony. With Singapore and Malaysia approaching independence, it was generally assumed that Britain's day was over and that Britain must withdraw, literally as well as formally, when the Union Jack was lowered for good over Government House. Edinger, on the contrary, believed that once independence had freed both sides from a relationship which inevitably generated frictions of all kinds, it would be easy, and very desirable, to create a new relationship, a more easy-going and spontaneous one. He believed, in short, that when the time came for Britain to hand over political responsibility to her former dependencies, she should be thinking not in terms of 'pulling out' but rather of going in on a different basis, of looking for fresh openings and planning fresh initiatives, whose essential foundation would be the acknowledgment of absolute equality of status between what would now be the two partners in a joint venture.

This in itself was interesting to Dickson; what made it music in his ears was the second part of Edinger's thesis, in which he suggested that in making this kind of new departure in human relations there was a special opportunity for the younger generation of Englishmen. Analysing what had gone wrong with the relationship between Britain and the subject peoples of the old empire, Edinger remarked that the social barriers which had arisen between the governors and the governed had been unknown to the architects of the empire, to men like Stamford Raffles in Singapore, Clive and the Lawrence brothers in India, James Brooke in Sarawak. These barriers had appeared because later generations of imperialists had grown pompous and distant, isolating themselves in their exclusive clubs and compounds from the indigenous life around them. Edinger quoted Sir John Glubb as saying, on his return from a life's work in the middle east, that Asia in the nineteen-fifties was 'taking her revenge on Britain, not for misrule but because we had arrogated to ourselves the position of a superior and privileged people on that

continent'. If the way to a better relationship lay through breaking down these barriers, who could be better qualified for the
task than the younger generation of Englishmen, in whom the old
impulses towards exploration and adventure still stirred but for
whom the old opportunities of advancement within the framework of imperial rule no longer existed?

Edinger's article gave Dickson just the encouragement he
needed. All that remained was to cut through the obstacles of
public apathy and official mistrust – and this was precisely the
kind of challenge that Dickson most enjoyed. He was presently
to find that there were other allies at hand, and meanwhile events
provided an unexpected opportunity for the experiment he had in
mind: the government decided that compulsory military service
should be discontinued in Britain. The decision posed far-reaching problems, especially for universities already overcrowded and
now faced with the prospect of a 'double intake', in the shape
of those who had just completed their military service and those
who no longer had to undertake it before going on to higher
studies. The implications of this soon preoccupied many people
who concerned themselves with the problems of the younger
generation and set them thinking along lines not dissimilar from
those on which Dickson's mind was working. But before he had
time to explore the possibilities of cooperation, Dickson was off
again, this time to Sarawak (where his brother was Director of
Education) on a journey which further sharpened the point of his
resolve.

Of this journey Dickson's wife Mora has given an engaging
account in her book *A Season in Sarawak*. Travelling by Land
Rover, on foot, or in canoes up the great rivers which alone gave
access to the hinterland of Sarawak, the Dicksons enjoyed hospitality in the longhouses of the Dayaks and found there a pattern
of living primitive in its superficial aspect, but fundamentally
coherent and satisfying. Life in a longhouse, wrote Mrs. Dickson,
'was an integrated whole from the cradle to the grave, and the
survival of the group depended on each unit fulfilling its unique
functions'. Young and old alike had their specific responsibilities

and it seemed to the Dicksons, when they compared the lot of the young Dayaks with that of their contemporaries in Britain, that the Dayaks enjoyed one clear advantage. Poor they might be, with a range of opportunity inescapably limited; but they retained something that the young Englishmen of the 'fifties as clearly lacked: 'a sense of their own place in the framework of living and of the duties and importance of that place'. What was the use of giving to our young citizens every material and educational advantage if we denied them the satisfaction (without which the rest remained merely tantalising) of being valued for what they could contribute to the community? There was something that we in our sophistication seemed to have forgotten, but which the Dayaks knew by instinct: that you only produce responsible citizens by giving them responsibility.

This was one half of the picture in Sarawak. The other side was more shadowed with uncertainties. With all its serene advantages, the Dayak pattern of living was plainly threatened by the onslaught of the twentieth century. On the first of their journeys to the interior of Sarawak, the Dicksons travelled by road for forty miles out of the capital, Kuching. Then the road gave out and the party went on on foot – passing as they did so a tractor nibbling at the jungle, thrusting aside the trees and clearing a path for the road's eventual extension. In time that road would run clear through from Kuching to the Indonesian border, a symbol of progress and expanded opportunity which would also, and inevitably, bring in its wake problems inherent in the disruption of an established social structure. How could the Dayaks on their own negotiate the transition from the old world to the new? Would it be possible for them, without sacrificing what was best in their own way of life, to accept and assimilate the advantages which the outside world had to offer?

The problem had already been foreseen and Mrs. Dickson has described the devoted attempts which were being made to ease the transition. Here again was an opportunity for youth – and another link in the chain of experience which led to the creation of Voluntary Service Overseas. Of the first volunteers who were to leave Britain a year later, six went to settlements visited by the Dicksons in the course of their 'Season in Sarawak'.

* * * *

The postwar development of the welfare state had not killed the impulse towards voluntary service; but it had made it harder to see where the remaining needs lay and what the precise objectives should be. The international work-camp movement, pioneered by International Voluntary Service (a branch of Service Civil International, whose headquarters were in Geneva) and encouraged by the United Nations Association, had explored one useful outlet. Oxfam and the Freedom from Hunger campaign were two practical expressions of the same urge, and in 1957 there were all sorts of other organisations looking, from slightly different angles, at the twin problems of development and community service, at the needs and the potentialities of a society rich in resources but ill-adapted to make those resources available where they were most needed. The approaching end of conscription for military service gave a fresh spur to such activities and a committee, under the chairmanship of Sir Ronald Adam, was examining the possibilities of joint action when Alec Dickson and his wife returned from Sarawak. Dickson joined in their discussions and travelled the country speaking to young audiences, testing the climate of opinion among those whose collaboration was vital if his ideas were to come to anything. He found an eager acceptance of those ideas and a positive hunger on the part of the young for an opportunity both to prove themselves and to play a part in the construction of a new world, a world in which theories of social and international cooperation would at last have some reality.

Official attitudes remained cautious, but Dickson was persistent (some of the officials whom he pestered might call this an understatement) and early in 1958 he found an ally and an opening which together did much to forward his initiative. The ally was Dr. Launcelot Fleming, then Bishop of Portsmouth (and now of Norwich), who himself had a close interest in youth's problems and was in fact chairman of the Church of England Youth Council. Dr. Fleming was exercised about the position of boys leaving

47

school and whose entry to the university would be delayed by the bottleneck created by the sudden ending of conscription. Himself an adventurous traveller in his youth, he was eager to devise means of occupying these school-leavers which would save them from boredom and inactivity. His interest in the kind of solution Dickson proposed was sharpened by his recognition that Dickson possessed the driving force needed to jolt an apathetic society into action. He and Dickson collaborated on the preparation of a letter which the Bishop signed and which was published in *The Sunday Times* on March 23rd, 1958. An anonymous sub-editor added the simple and appropriate headline 'The Year Between'.

In that letter Dr. Fleming invited the readers of *The Sunday Times* to consider four main propositions. First, he suggested that the under-developed countries of the Commonwealth offered 'opportunities of service that would not only make a positive contribution to those countries but would constitute an experience of inestimable benefit to many of our young people'. This was the overall concept, of a venture with a dual purpose, offering service where it was needed and a sense of purpose to those equipped to provide it. Second, as to the type of service, the letter instanced primary and adult education, youth work, community development and social welfare – adding that the kind of projects envisaged 'do not postulate specialist skills so much as a readiness to work alongside the local people'. This was a further important element in Dickson's thinking, echoing the ideas that George Edinger had advanced in *The Spectator:* the emphasis was to be firmly on cooperation between equals, as opposed to the more didactic approach proper to the 'expert' imparting his specialised knowledge. Third came the Bishop's immediate preoccupation, the need to find 'for the best of our young people' something useful as well as exciting to do in the difficult transition period between leaving school and entering university or embarking on a career. Here there were echoes too of the Sarawak experience, of that vision of the secure framework of a community in which each element and each age-group had its agreed sphere of responsibility, where none was excluded or left to rust in idleness and frustration.

6. Science teaching in Malawi

7
A physiotherapist
working in Malawi

8. A cadet volunteer surveying in New Guinea

9. A medical volunteer in Papua

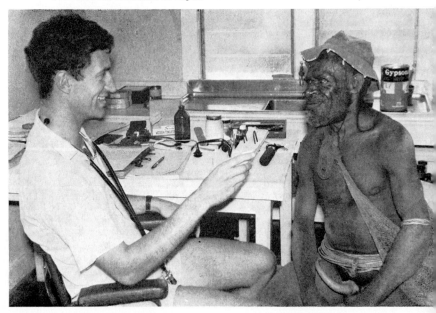

Finally, the letter touched on the practical problem of creating an organisation which would handle the logistics of such a venture, selecting the candidates, finding worth-while jobs for them to do, raising the money to send them overseas and ensuring that at the other end there would be someone to meet them and make proper use of their services. None of this would be easy, and unless it was done and done well the scheme would never get off the ground.

Looking back now, it is astonishing to realise that within six months of the publication of Dr. Fleming's letter the first volunteers were on their way. It was not that the difficulties suddenly evaporated, or that the new initiative at once captured the imagination of an awakened British public – far from it. The result was due to several closely related causes, whose unifying factor was the energy and determination of Alec Dickson.

Of the difficulties that had to be faced, the principal one was not financial, important though that was, nor yet organisational, for it soon became apparent that plenty of individuals saw the merit of such a scheme and were prepared to work hard to launch it. The real barrier to be surmounted was psychological. It was, as Dickson himself has put it, 'the difficulty of changing attitudes in people's minds'. The scheme went against the grain of contemporary thinking at so many points. There was the official mind, cautious, mistrustful of amateurs meddling on the fringes of professional territory, anxious above all to avoid becoming involved in new and perhaps complicated commitments abroad. There was the public mind, in which domestic and material preoccupations, combined with a sense of Britain's diminished stature in the world, seemed to have extinguished our native enterprise. There was the mind of the younger generation, as always a puzzle to its elders, who were bewildered by the evidence of youth's waywardness and failed, not unnaturally, to interpret it as simply a part of youth's search for an identity and a sense of purpose. At all these levels there was a need for a change of attitude if the new scheme was to enjoy the bare minimum of public support.

The letter to *The Sunday Times* set things moving. The response to it confirmed that there were opportunities abroad and revealed a wide measure of support among headmasters in Britain. Provided now with a clear blue-print for action, the various bodies cooperating on Sir Ronald Adam's committee contributed support and ideas, out of which was gradually extemporised a pattern of organisation. Janet Lacey of Inter-Christian Aid provided office space and an embryonic secretariat, where Geoffrey Clark dealt briskly with a growing bulk of correspondence. And Alec Dickson himself, in the intervals of selecting volunteers, arranging their destinations and the means of reaching them, pressing his scheme in official quarters and handling almost the whole of its administration, went canvassing energetically for the funds which could set the scheme in motion.

Whatever the response in terms of support and enthusiasm, without money – and quite a lot of it – the idea had no future. And more than this, money was in a sense the touchstone of public approval. It was one thing to write in support of the scheme, quite another to put £500 into launching it. There was no suggestion that public money would be forthcoming, although the idea of voluntary service overseas now had a useful friend in Alan Lennox-Boyd, the Secretary for Commonwealth Relations. It was to the charitable trusts and one or two of the largest commercial firms in the country that Dickson turned his attention. Not all of them were easily convinced that this was an enterprise worth supporting, but by the late summer of 1958 Dr. Fleming, as treasurer, had received enough contributions to make it possible to send out fourteen volunteers. They went to Nigeria, Ghana and Sarawak and no one knew quite what to call them, for the name VSO had not yet been coined. They went as part of an organisation temporarily called 'The Year Between', and they were the advance guard, the pathfinders for the thousands who were to follow now that the first step had been taken.

For those fourteen pioneers, the remaining months of 1958 were full of excitement as they explored horizons new to them both literally and figuratively. For those who had sent them on their way there was no chance to relax, as they waited to hear how the experiment was working out in practice. All sorts of problems of organisation and administration called out for answers. More requests for volunteers were coming in, more enquiries from schools where masters and pupils alike were interested in the new enterprise. There were leaflets to be written and printed, accounts to be kept, correspondence to be answered. The 1958 operation was under way; the 1959 follow-up had to be planned and set in train. Above all, now that the scheme had been started, now that the idea had become a fact, it was plain that there must be some more clear-cut form of organisation, if only because the strain on Dickson and his tiny band of collaborators threatened to overwhelm them.

The question was: what sort of organisation was right for a scheme which had no precedents and which owed its existence, in part at least, precisely to Dickson's wish to avoid identification with more formally constituted bodies working in the same field? Presumably it must have a constitution, but Dickson had no use for the predictable type of semi-statutory body so dear to the English, with a superannuated colonial governor at its head and a high-powered council whose experience might range over five continents and fifty years of old-fashioned administration – but whose members would know little of the new impulses stirring, either in Britain or in the territories moving towards independence. Such a body might be able to exert a useful amount of influence in Whitehall; it would certainly have advantages when it came to fund-raising. But how closely could it reflect the purpose of the new undertaking and how effective (this was the crucial question) would be its appeal, both to those who might wish to volunteer and to those who thought of employing them?

The question was debated during the remaining months of 1958 – which saw the first year's complement of eighteen volunteers completed by the dispatch of four more – and in the end a small Council was appointed with John Marsh, the director of the Industrial Welfare Society, as chairman. The name 'Voluntary Service Overseas' was formally adopted and Alec Dickson was given the title of Project Adviser, while Geoffrey Clark continued somehow to keep his head above water as an overworked Secretary. Working closely with Inter-Church Aid,[1] and from ICA's headquarters in Eaton Gate, this triumvirate handled all the affairs of the infant organisation during the first exciting stage of its existence. How they did it now seems a mystery, but their success meant that a more formal approach to the constitutional niceties could be postponed until it was possible to see how the scheme was working out in practice. The ship had been launched; now the problem was to keep it afloat.

[1] Which later changed its name to Christian Aid.

Chapter 4

The Advance-Guard

It is easy to imagine the impatience with which Dickson and his colleagues waited for news of the pioneers. Had the travel arrangements worked smoothly and had the boys arrived safely at their scattered destinations? Would they fit easily into the life of the local community? How well would they adapt themselves to unfamiliar conditions, food, climate, conventions? The question marks were endless, and they all indicated aspects of the same two fundamental questions: had the volunteers been well chosen, and would they be able to give VSO the initial impetus which would set it firmly on its course?

The answers were not long in coming and before Christmas Dickson was able to put together a news-sheet, made up of extracts from the volunteers' letters, which must have been enormously encouraging to all those who had helped to launch the scheme. To begin with, there was the tone of almost incredulous delight in which, with hardly an exception, the boys wrote on the new life which had enveloped them. 'I am absolutely taken with the scheme and the people here, and love every minute of my work', wrote one from Sarawak, while another could hardly wait to say that 'from the start Sarawak, and this job in particular, is the epitome of my wildest dreams come true . . .', and a third, looking round him in Nigeria, mused in happy bewilderment: 'to think that I might have been working in an office.'

Apart from anything else, of course, there was the sheer

excitement and stimulus of new experience, of an exploration in time as well as space which took the volunteers far off the beaten track of their orderly Western environment. The pair posted to the Man o'War Bay centre, situated, as one of them described it, 'on an old banana plantation, with thick rain-forest surrounding it and coming right down to the sea', only reached their final destination after a journey from Lagos which lasted a month and included 150 miles on foot through an undeveloped area of Eastern Nigeria. This was only an introduction, but it opened windows enough, as one of them made clear in describing his first impressions: 'Ilorin, where the Emir received us and the night market was an unforgettable sight; Bida, famous for its brass and glass: the Plateau itself, with its rolling grassland and outcrops of rocks, and where we met Fulani herdsmen – colourful, striking people but very shy, though eventually we did gain their confidence. We were calling at villages and seeing sights that the average Nigerian would never see.'

From Sarawak, another wrote in the same vein of his expeditions with the boys from a Dayak settlement: 'Sometimes we have got hold of a boat and paddled up-river, sometimes we have walked to more distant longhouses or simply gone into the forests on joint hunting expeditions. The boys are amazingly sure-footed.... I have been instructed in the use of the blow-pipe and casting-net.'

This kind of thing was irresistible – but as the letters came in, with their picturesque stamps and the improbable-sounding postmarks, much more began to emerge. There was news, not only from the volunteers themselves, but from those for whom they had gone to work, from the Principal of the Man o'War Bay Training Centre, the Headmaster of a secondary school in Ghana, the Director of a social research institute in Northern Rhodesia, from the Bishop of Borneo and the men in charge of the various community development schemes to which volunteers had been attached in Sarawak. From their comments and from those of the boys themselves it was soon evident that all sorts of hopes were being fulfilled, that the ideas which had looked visionary to some, and downright impractical to others, were working out in practice – and that these pathfinders were likely to create a demand for more volunteers which the London end of VSO would have to work hard to meet. The Government of Northern Rhodesia wrote to ask for six more 'as soon as possible' to work with District Commissioners in the field and to help in schemes for African education, youth training and probation. Two of the volunteers at a community development centre in Sarawak made themselves so useful that within three months the man in charge was writing to say that 'we could use another half dozen lads if they were available'. From elsewhere the story was the same and a British administrative officer at Enugu in Eastern Nigeria observed: 'I know what inspired the launching of this scheme, but I think something may have been wrought of even greater significance than perhaps even you dared to hope.'

There is not much doubt that what he said was true, or at least that the success of those first volunteers brought into much sharper focus ideas which, until these young men put them to the test, were inevitably uncertain and a little fuzzy at the edges. For one thing, it is in the nature of a novel idea that it should be imprecise, as a draughtsman's first sketch is tentative; waiting, as it must, for its full development, on the creative interaction of imagination and reality. And then the ideas which went into VSO had been gathered from here and there and were the distillation of much thought and discussion among a number of people. Each of these must have seen the ultimate objective in subtly different terms, emphasising now this and now that aspect of a generally agreed purpose. Even Dickson, whose original concept had remained the essential core of the whole idea, had refined and modified and developed it in his dealings with his collaborators and he can no more have been certain than they were of the exact shape and significance it would assume when it was translated into action. From my own experience the nearest parallel I can think of is the writing of a television script, which can never be the 'final' version so long as it remains on paper; it can achieve life and finality only when the producer transforms it into words and pictures on the living screen.

What did begin to emerge, as the outlines grew firmer, as the volunteers and their hosts took stock of each other, was the central fact that in this wholly original experiment in human relations there was not one side that gave and another that received. The benefits were mutual. If the volunteers were able to contribute something that was needed – and it was very soon apparent that they were – it was equally apparent that they themselves were gaining with every moment spent in their new environment and in the exercise of qualities and aptitudes which some of them had scarcely suspected in themselves. Indeed, it was remarkable how closely the experience of the volunteers mirrored the hopes of those who had helped to send them on their way. 'I came here thinking I was going to teach', remarked a boy far up the Baram River in Sarawak; 'I now realise I shall learn far more than I will ever teach.' And that concept of 'The Year Between' received graphic justification from one of his colleagues teaching at another remote settlement among the Dayaks. 'The year or so after you leave school', he wrote, 'is an absolutely vital time in the life of anyone. It is then that you must really come to grips with yourself and sort out your values for the future. This type of work has certainly taught me in a very short while which things to value in life and I have before me the shining example of some remarkable men. In such a worthwhile job as this you surely get a better sense of perspective than in some "filling-in-the-gap" job at home.'

A mature comment, that, for someone who had been a schoolboy six months before; and it gives an idea of what a hothouse this new life could be, where all a boy's energies were absorbed in the service of a community as different as could be from anything he had ever experienced before. A community, too, in which he had a particular role, a function for which he had been picked, after careful scrutiny by men five thousand miles away, who had sent him here in the confidence that he could supply what was needed. A community, again, finite and assured in its attitudes to life, less troubled by doubts and innovations than the society from which he sprang – which yet placed in him its confidence as a messenger from an outside world of which little was known, but much was expected. It would have been surprising if he had not sometimes, especially in the early days, felt anxious at the responsibility vested in him. It was perhaps less surprising that under the stimulus of that responsibility his natural qualities asserted themselves and that, with self-knowledge, he blossomed as rapidly as the tropical plants about him – into a man.

The process involved coming to terms with facts of life hitherto encountered, if at all, only in the guise of social theory. A volunteer who had gone as a social research worker to Northern Rhodesia looked up one day from a display of tribal dancing to see a Viscount of Central African Airways passing overhead. With surprise he realised that it was the flight that had brought him to Livingstone only a long week before, and when he sat down in the evening to write to London, he remarked that during that first week he had made a number of friends among the boys of the local secondary school. 'I am intending to spend Christmas with three of them', he wrote, 'camping on the banks of the Zambesi near the Victoria Falls. I am eagerly looking forward to that experience. I will just add that we shall have to take and cook our own food, since there is nowhere where they and I can eat in the same building.'

After a month the same volunteer was writing: 'It is strange to think that four weeks ago I did not know anyone in the whole of Central Africa; I seem to have made more friends this month than in the other 19 years of my life.' One African friend had been staying with him, to the astonishment of the rest of the little community; 'as you can see, such things are just unheard of in this part of the world . . . it is a great advantage to be able to meet Africans as an equal'.

In Ghana it was the same story. A boy teaching at a secondary school wrote: 'We have here a much more friendly relationship with Ghanaians than most young people in the large towns appear to have. There is certainly room for more young teachers here – it seems easier for us to be on equal terms with the pupils, who like to be taught by people of their own age.'

Here was the idea which George Edinger had thrown out in his *Spectator* article coming to fruition. Ghana had just become independent. Its people had elected to remain within the Commonwealth – but the transition from a condition of dependence to one of equality with Britain was bound to be difficult, and the difficulty could only be overcome in the end by personal contacts of a wholly new and different kind. It was too much to expect of those Englishmen whose experience was of the old relationship that they should all, and immediately, adjust their outlook to suit the needs of the new. It was natural that Ghanaians, sensitive about their new dignity and mindful of past resentments, should be suspicious of men whose status – however sincerely they tried to modify it – remained outwardly indistinguishable from that of the former colonial masters. But a young man coming fresh from school, unused to authority and unhampered by any concept of superiority, could bridge this gap without effort and with no sense on either side of condescension. It was the first and fundamental justification of the new approach.

For the volunteers to be able to make friends, to communicate, was vitally important; but of course, by itself, it was not enough. If VSO was to make its mark, its advocates had to show that it could do more than oil the wheels of a society in transition. Its usefulness in this sense must be complementary to its main function of helping to get things done, of providing – at little cost and with no thought of a *quid pro quo* – some of the motive force for progress. By its nature its pretensions must be modest. Mustering its forces among the young and inexperienced, the temptation was not open to it of trying to change the face of the world. What it could offer, must offer, was a few extra shoulders to the wheel and a willingness to deploy its energies where they could best be used, either because the need was greatest or because other and more sophisticated instruments of progress were not to hand.

It was with these thoughts in mind that the projects for this first year had been chosen. In each case the volunteers had been sent to work, under the supervision of other Englishmen, in posts where an extra pair of hands and a fresh, eager, enquiring mind could make all the difference to the effectiveness of a local scheme for education or community development. One which combined both was the Budu project in Sarawak, a cooperative settlement organised and administered by a devoted Scotsman, John Wilson (the Bishop of Borneo once described him as an 'agnostic saint'), in a group of villages far up the Krian River. Briefly, Wilson's idea in establishing the scheme had been to equip this small community of Dayak villagers for the challenge that lay ahead of them: the challenge of adapting their traditional way of life to the new pattern creeping up on them as Sarawak entered the twentieth century. This involved familiarising them with some of the simpler techniques of the outside world; with the uses, for instance, of a money economy, to enable them to hold their own with those who might otherwise have exploited them. In short, it involved education, but an education strictly adapted to the needs of this particular community and planned, as far as possible, to ensure that the old ways and the new should meet and merge, rather than collide.[1]

Alec Dickson knew Wilson and had visited Budu the year before, when his plans for a volunteer scheme were still in the formative stage. He had seen here the ideal type of opening for the boys he hoped to recruit, where there was a real job to be done in an environment which could not fail to capture the imagination of any alert and sensitive young man; a job, too, whose successful accomplishment would depend, not on experience or expertise, but on bringing sympathy and enthusiasm to bear on the fulfilment of plans already carefully laid. It seemed, indeed, the ideal testing ground.

For the two volunteers chosen to make the trial, it proved much more than that. The journey up the river by canoe was exciting; and Budu itself, a clearing in the jungle, with school, dispensary and cooperative store flanking the Dayak longhouse, was a new world, physically circumscribed but rich in the promise

[1] A full and fascinating account of the Budu Development Scheme is contained in Mora Dickson's *A Season in Sarawak*.

of self-fulfilment. Above all, from the moment of their arrival there could be no mistake about the fact that they were needed. Wilson set them at once to learn Dayak, made it plain – and it was this more than anything that lent flavour to the adventure – that as soon as they had found their feet, responsibility would be thrust upon them.

And so it was. Within a matter of weeks one of them was writing 'I am here on my own at Enkiliki (one of the subsidiary villages in the Budu scheme) – in charge of a primary school, the Co-operative shop, a rubber plantation and the dispensary. . . .' With enthusiasm he described the methods he used in teaching the Dayak boys, work which he found 'tremendously rewarding and enjoyable' because they were so eager to learn; and his delight in his own good fortune was almost audible as he went on to say how at the week-ends he went up to the central village to organise the distribution of stores to the five villages. 'The boys take me up-river to Nanga Budu, driving the boats up three quite dangerous sets of rapids and several small ones, all of which involve real fights to keep the boat afloat (especially when it is heavily loaded with valuable stores).' In nonchalant parenthesis he added that these week-end trips meant that 'I do meet one white man a week, anyway'.

When Wilson showed his confidence in them like this, by leaving them in charge while he went off to launch a school or a new training scheme in another part of the area, they had the satisfaction of realising that their coming had made a difference, that the success of the whole enterprise now rested in part on them. This was confirmed by Wilson himself, when he wrote after three months to tell VSO: 'Both are giving a service that money could not repay. . . . Their presence and help have allowed a quicker progress to take place and even now I view their departure next September with misgivings and wonder just how we ever managed to get on without them.'

It was above all this sense of being valued, of having a real job of work to do which would otherwise have remained undone, that stimulated the volunteers and kept their energies from flagging in the unfamiliar climate of the tropics. From Ghana one of them described his working day, which started with p.t. at 5.30 in the morning and went on through a full programme of classroom teaching, games and such things as amateur dramatics, until lights out at 9.45 p.m. – and remarked: 'This is quite a strenuous timetable and during school time there is certainly plenty of work to be done. It is, however, absorbingly interesting and there is never a dull moment. Only perhaps on Friday morning, when you are teaching your twentieth period of simple English to boys whose average age is roughly 21 but who are in Form Two, do you begin to flag a little. Yet they are very keen to learn, are always begging for extra lessons, and slacking is extremely rare. . . .'

For the two volunteers acting as auxiliary instructors at the Man o'War Bay centre in Nigeria, the day was equally full, with the emphasis on the physical activities of a course modelled on that of the Outward Bound schools in Britain. A week of general training in activities like seamanship, swimming and first aid was followed by two weeks of expeditions which worked up gradually to the climax of an assault on the 13,000 foot peak of Mount Cameroon. Here the value of the practical accomplishments learned earlier was put to a wider test involving the spirit as well as the muscles of both trainees and instructors. 'We found', wrote one of the volunteers at the end of the first of these courses, 'that the great problem was not the physical one of climbing the mountain, but the psychological one of persuading the students that the feat was possible. "I shall die" and "It pains me too much" were common expressions, and we had to exert ourselves to the utmost to encourage them. The mountain lived up to all that had been said of it, and certainly separated the sheep from the goats.' If the students were tested, so were their youthful instructors, and the Principal of Man o'War wrote to VSO: 'There is no doubt that both these young men have given and are giving most valuable service. I am still one member of my permanent staff short, and with the growing tempo of events in Nigeria[1] and the diminishing number of senior officers available

[1] Nigeria was due to achieve independence less than two years later.

to assist locally, the help of two extra responsible staff has been of great benefit, both to me and to the students.'

Praising the energy and adaptability of the volunteers, the Principal remarked that they had fitted easily into the busy pattern of life at the Centre, and he added a comment that chimed in with the observations of many of the volunteers themselves. 'They have mixed naturally with the Africans', he wrote, 'and being of the same age as the students on some courses they had many things in common, despite the great difference in education and background. I would like to add that I consider the choice of these two young men an excellent one – and I hope that should the scheme develop from these small beginnings the future quality of volunteer will be as high as that of these pioneers.'

Here was the challenge for the future. It was plain before this first year was half way through that the scheme was proving a success, that there were jobs and to spare which needed doing and for which these young enthusiasts were ideally. fitted. There was no doubt either of the benefits which the volunteers themselves were deriving from the experience, in terms of maturity and self-assurance, of that wider awareness of the attitudes of others which is fundamental to a liberal outlook, and of an understanding of the forces at work in the rapidly changing world into which they were growing up. The question was, could the organisers of VSO be sure of maintaining the high standard which these path-finders had set – and, beyond that, would it be possible so to expand and develop the organisation itself as to cope with the much larger number that seemed likely to apply and for whom work could certainly be found?

In a sense, this next stage was the critical one in the history of VSO. The first heave was over, the initial difficulties had been overcome, the scheme was airborne. It was no mean achievement – but to keep it going might be even harder, involving a steady slog at the problems of administration and an ability to rouse enthusiasm for an idea no longer shiningly new and visionary. To create something out of nothing is exhilarating and calls for particular qualities of enterprise and imagination. To maintain and develop something that already exists may be equally exacting but less inspiring; certainly it demands different and steadier qualities, of application and a concern for the routine detail, whose exercise offers less obvious scope for initiative. If the volunteers had been tested, so now were the organisers of VSO.

Essentially, the problems of the next stage boiled down to two. There was the question of organisation, which in effect had been shelved when Inter-Church Aid had agreed to see VSO through the first two years of its existence: and there was the financial question. Of the two, the second was the more straightforward.

Budget statements do not make exciting reading, but it is perhaps of interest to glance for a moment at the earliest surviving document in the financial history of VSO. It is contained on a single sheet of notepaper and it details the costs, for the twelve months ending on June 9th, 1959, of the original 'Sarawak scheme', the nucleus of that first year's operations, under which eight volunteers were to be sent (two more were added towards the end of 1958) to projects under the aegis of the Sarawak Department of Education. The account, drawn up by the Bishop of Portsmouth acting in his capacity as Treasurer (a bishop, it seems – and it is an intriguing sidelight – has the legal status of a corporation), records receipts, from charitable trusts and other benefactors, of £4600. Expenditure, at approximately £4450, left a working balance for the following year of £153 8s. 7d. In other words, it had cost VSO about £550 a head to send these eight young men to Sarawak – and the next most significant detail that emerges is that no less than £2994, or almost exactly two-thirds of the total expenditure, had gone on fares. There were no payments for salaries, since VSO as yet had no salaried officials or employees. There was an item of £20 for insurance to cover the volunteers against sickness and accident, and payments totalling some £207 for the costs of administration in Britain. Otherwise all the rest of the money, a total of £1200, had been spent on the subsistence costs of the volunteers while they were overseas.

These figures provided some important guidelines for the

future. If each volunteer was to cost VSO £550, and if plans to expand the number of volunteers to fifty a year, or even a hundred, came to fruition, it was going to be necessary to raise some very large sums of money.[1] Of these sums, the larger part would go on fares, unless some cheaper way could be found of transporting volunteers than by the ordinary commercial air and sea routes; and in 1959 successful efforts were made to persuade shipping companies to provide free passages. Finally – and this tied up with the other main problem, of devising the proper form of organisation for VSO now that it was a going concern – the question must presently arise, especially if there was to be a substantial increase in numbers, of adding to the costs by taking on a salaried staff. And this was not any longer a simple matter of choice; it was becoming one of necessity, since the hard-pressed 'triumvirate' which was doing all the work[2] was in danger of collapsing under the strain.

A problem within a problem was that of finding time to consider the question of organisation, while at the same time keeping the scheme in motion. There was no neat dividing line between one year's operation and the next, no off-season in which Dickson and his colleagues could sit back and chew the cud of reminiscence or self-congratulation. The volunteers in the field needed attention – this was a point on which Dickson was insistent, and it has remained the ambition of VSO always to retain personal and regular contact with each individual volunteer – but meanwhile the early efforts to arouse interest in the scheme, combined with the success of the first volunteers, had brought in a stream of enquiries. They came from would-be volunteers and from those who wanted to acquire them, as well as from headmasters and other interested people who had got wind of the scheme and wanted to hear more about it. Before 1958 was out the 1959 scheme was taking shape, and as the new year un-

[1] In effect the cost per volunteer was steadily reduced as the organisation expanded. It is now calculated at £370 for every school-leaver volunteer and £500 for a graduate.

[2] See last para. of Ch. 3.

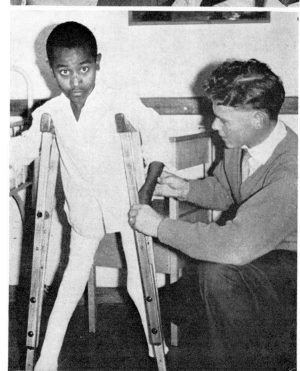

10
English teaching
in Laos

11
Ethiopia:
crutches designed and
fitted by an ex-apprentice
volunteer

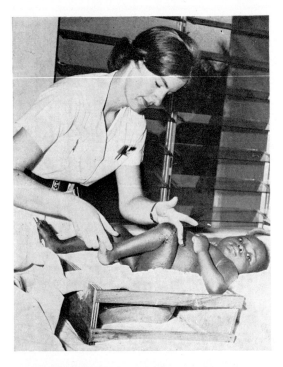

12
Nigeria: a medical volunteer
at a teaching hospital
in Lagos

13
A technical volunteer
instructing engineering
students in Sarawak

folded it became apparent that unless VSO was prepared to turn down many of the opportunities which it had itself brought into the open, expansion was not merely possible, it was virtually inevitable.

In the end the eighteen volunteers who had gone out in 1958 were succeeded by sixty in 1959. These went to eighteen countries and to a wider variety of projects. Among them were the first two girls to serve with VSO, to whose adventurous spirit a tribute is due in passing, and they also included four ex-apprentices from industry, who opened up a fruitful new field of activity of which there will be more to say in due time. But these innovations and this expansion were only achieved by efforts on the part of the Chairman, John Marsh, the Projects Director, Alec Dickson, and the Secretary, Geoffrey Clarke, which it would have been unreasonable to ask any of them to repeat. The time had come to move confidently out of the stage of experiment and improvisation and to set VSO on a firmer base, providing it with the structure – and the permanent staff – which would enable it to function with assurance and without strain on a wider scale.

All this was made easier by the support which the government now gave to VSO, and which reflected the interest taken in it from the start by the Secretary for Commonwealth Relations, Alan Lennox-Boyd, as well as the fact that the government could not ignore the arrival on the scene of an entity which was bound to affect, in however small a measure, Britain's dealings with the emergent countries. In 1959, when VSO had successfully financed its first year's operations and was looking about for the means to support an expanded follow-up programme, the government produced a grant, from the fund for Colonial Development and Welfare, of £9000. In addition, the R.A.F. helped with the transport of volunteers and this, together with the offer of free passages from a number of steamship lines, meant that out of the sixty volunteers who went overseas in 1959 more than half were carried at no cost to VSO. The saving, on the heaviest item of expenditure in VSO's budget, was a most welcome relief and together with the Colonial Development grant it gave the organisers of VSO the opportunity to think in altogether new terms about the future.

At the end of 1959 the Chairman summarised the position and listed the possibilities. The scheme had been functioning successfully for a year and a half, there were sixty volunteers in the field, and 'there is no doubt that the actual operation of sending boys and girls overseas has been very rewarding to all concerned, to the young people themselves, to the hosts, to the sponsors and parents'. By the middle of 1960 Inter-Church Aid would have fulfilled its undertaking to see VSO through its first two years. It was now necessary for the committee to choose between four courses which the Chairman suggested were open to it. They could ask Janet Lacey and the ICA to continue to administer the scheme for another two years. They could propose to the Royal Commonwealth Society – which had taken a close interest from the start and of which Alec Dickson was a staff member – that the RCS should take over administrative and financial responsibility for VSO. They could look about for some other existing organisation which might take VSO under its wing. Or, finally, they could burn their boats and decide to establish VSO as a separate and independent organisation, with its own constitution, its own articles of association, its own paid staff and all the administrative accoutrements that they would need.

The Chairman, John Marsh, added that he personally thought it would be unwise to take the last course, since 'it would entail a tremendous amount of work and would prove a costly business at a time when we have no promise of a continuing income of any kind'.

The question of costs was now a central one. So far it had been possible to keep them very low, partly because Dickson and his helpers had put in a great deal of voluntary work, and partly because most of the routine administrative work had been done by ICA as an extension of its normal operations and without charge. It would be wrong for the committee to plan for the future on the assumption that either of these conditions would continue to apply; and there could be no question of large-scale expansion while they did. In short, the decision which now faced the committee was a crucial one, on which hung the whole question of the future of VSO and of whether the idea which it embodied was to be allowed to realise its full potential. It was no less than a vote of confidence, and one which had to be taken, not in the dark, certainly, for there was plenty of evidence of goodwill and support for VSO, but with very little concrete evidence that the conditions for VSO's survival in fact existed.

It cannot have been an easy decision, and the balance of the practical arguments seemed to be in favour of caution. But then, if practical arguments were always to be allowed their full weight, at the expense of the kind of inspired guesswork that also had its place in the development of human society, an idea like Voluntary Service Overseas would never be allowed to get off the drawing board. In January of 1960 the committee took the plunge, constituted VSO as an independent organisation and set about recruiting for it a staff of its own. The budget estimates for 1960 showed that independence was still qualified, or rather that its maintenance for the time being rested in part on the continuing benevolence of friends like the Royal Commonwealth Society, which put at VSO's disposal office accommodation (three rooms, but it was enough) in return for a nominal rent of £10 a year. But the essential step was taken; sink or swim, VSO was now on its own.

Chapter 5

Towards a More Professional Approach

At the beginning of 1960 independence was very much in the air. One after another, the new nations of Africa and Asia were striking out on their own, in such rapid succession that it was becoming hard to keep track of the membership of the United Nations—and the old world, waking up to its responsibilities, tried to see that they got as good a start as possible. All sorts of initiatives in the field of international aid culminated in the idea of the 'sixties as a 'development decade', in which a concerted effort by rich and poor, developed and under-developed alike, should lift the whole world to a higher plane of well-being and cooperation.

Looking back now, it is easier to see the opportunities that were missed than the gains that were made, but at least there was the realisation that the problems existed and that they could best be tackled by a joint effort. The new nations were learning that independence was a fine word that buttered no parsnips: that once the fireworks and the celebrations were over and you settled down to daily life once more, things looked very much the same as they had done before – and certainly no easier. The retiring colonial power (and of course Britain was more closely concerned than anyone else in these changing relationships) realised that when one of your wards came of age, it was not enough to salute the new flag and bow yourself out with a good grace: if privileges came to an abrupt end, responsibilities tended to outlive them.

Nor was this a simple matter of *noblesse oblige*; it was also sound common sense, what you might call 'development logic'. For, with all its overtones of benevolence and humanitarianism, the theory of development aid was founded on the hard-headed proposition that the world's prosperity was indivisible, that the rich nations would benefit as well as the poor if poverty could be eliminated. It might be our moral duty to help our poorer neighbours; it was certainly the only way to put them in a position to help us by buying the goods we wanted to sell. In 1960 the thing was not often expressed as baldly as that – but that was what it amounted to when you came right down to it.

Because of all this, the idea of a corps of volunteers (who could in some small measure reinforce our efforts to provide aid) found support in some not always predictable places. As the experiment proved a success, the support increased – and the idea of sending volunteers to work in the developing countries spread, both in Britain and beyond. This was all to the good; but VSO was only one of many ideas, official and unofficial, practical and impractical, which were being floated about this time and which had in common the objective of building a new world out of the disintegration of the old. The appearance of each added one more to the already bewildering multiplicity of organisations known by their initials. There were the agencies of the United Nations: FAO and WHO. There were various bodies spawned by the Colonial Office and the CRO, such as the Colonial Development Corporation and the Overseas Service Aid Scheme; these tried to prevent the wholesale withdrawal of British colonial servants from territories which had ceased to be colonies, by transforming them into visiting 'experts'. The Department of Technical Cooperation was about to be formed, the chrysalis out of which would eventually emerge the Ministry of Overseas Development, with the function of coordinating these and other endeavours for providing aid to the developing countries. The British Council, from its original role as a purveyor of British culture, had developed into another vital component in the machinery of aid, since so often the kind of assistance needed by a nation struggling

69

to independence was with education, the fundamental passport to the wider realm of technical competence to which the new nations impatiently sought entry.

The fortunes of VSO were soon to become closely intertwined with those of the British Council, and it is of passing interest to record that at much the same moment that saw the birth of VSO the British Council was setting on foot a very similar experiment. The British Council scheme, which grew out of the same desire to find useful employment for boys leaving school and not yet able to take up places at overcrowded universities, originated with a telephone call from the officer in charge of recruitment for the Shell Company – and what is chiefly remarkable about it is the speed with which his initiative was followed up. At the end of April 1958 the Controller of Education for the British Council called a meeting to discuss the idea; less than four months later a group of volunteers were on their way to India and Pakistan. Not a bad achievement for an organisation which its critics tried to label as imprecise in its objectives and ponderously bureaucratic in its methods of operation – and one more indication of the mood of the times.

The British Council scheme ran for four years before it was merged, by mutual agreement, in the widening activities of VSO. During that time there was fairly close contact between the two organisations and general agreement on the objectives in view, though not always about the best method of achieving them. Alec Dickson was unsympathetic to the idea of mixing the volunteer concept with the necessarily more formal approach of the British Council; and when the Council in turn was trying to decide whether to maintain its own volunteer scheme or to hand over to VSO, doubts were expressed about 'the organising capacity of the present VSO set-up'.

There were the seeds there of future dissensions – but what was more important for the moment was the fact that the British Council and VSO become aware of each other, saw something of each other's methods of working, exchanged information and ideas and established in some cases personal connections which were later to prove valuable to both of them. There were Council officers – like Peter Marsh, who was given the task of setting the British Council scheme on its feet – who during subsequent tours of duty overseas found themselves in touch with the volunteers of VSO and showed themselves especially sympathetic to their aims and problems. And there were contacts with leading figures in the field of education, who were members of neither organisation but interested in both. Notable among these was Dr. Robert Birley, then Chairman of the Headmasters' Conference and nearing the end of his term as Headmaster of Eton, who joined the Council of VSO and played an important part in its future development.

The concept that found expression in VSO was new; the idea of voluntary service to the community, of course, was not, and there were other organisations in being before VSO came on the scene whose objectives were very similar. The oldest-established among them was one founded by Pierre Ceresole, a Swiss engineer, in the bitter aftermath of the first world war. Ceresole's idea was that since the armies of Europe had in a sense collaborated in the devastation of northern France and Belgium, it would be appropriate that a peaceful army, made up once more of contingents from many nations, should repair the material damage and in doing so try to heal the spiritual wounds which Europe had inflicted on herself. Ceresole called his army Service Civil International, and the idea gained ground, spreading eventually far beyond Europe until there were more than twenty branches all over the world. When the immediate task of making the battlefields of Europe habitable again was over, SCI turned its attention to other, more enduring, examples of human failure: to the relief of poverty, the provision of medical care, always with this underlying idea of international cooperation, of providing help that ignored frontiers of all kinds and recognised only a human need. Earthquakes, epidemics, the perennial disasters which for most of us are remote headlines, were for the voluntary workers of SCI opportunities, not only to relieve suffering but also to demonstrate human solidarity. International Voluntary Service, the British branch of

71

SCI, played a part in the rebuilding of Skopje, sent nurses, builders, plumbers to help in caring for the refugees from the war of independence in Algeria; but it did not, and does not, overlook the humbler, the more humdrum challenge of daily misfortune at home. For every one of its volunteers who goes to work for a year or two on one of these major projects there are many who spend a couple of weeks, or even a week-end, attending to the plight of the disabled, the pensioner, the unfortunates left shivering in the corridors of the welfare state.

A similar spirit of internationalism animated the work of the United Nations Association in Britain, and it too, among its many other activities, recruited volunteers and sent them overseas to work mainly on behalf of the special agencies of the UN. Indeed, there were some who thought that the whole concept of voluntary service belonged properly under the wing of the United Nations, where it could be developed without any suspicion of chauvinism or national self-interest. Ideally this might be true, but the practical objections are formidable. There is the obvious difficulty presented by problems of language and of cooperation at a practical level between individuals accustomed to widely different methods and standards. Then again, it is in the nature of a volunteer programme that it should be able to operate as simply and as swiftly as possible, if only because the volunteers are bound to be people with little time to spare. If they can afford a year, or possibly two, between one stage and the next of their careers, it is vital to make the fullest use of that time, to see that no more of it than is necessary is spent in bureaucratic preliminaries. No one who has any experience of working for a United Nations agency, which is the servant of more than a hundred masters, would minimise the difficulty of getting prompt decisions out of such a body. So the idea of a United Nations volunteer corps on any substantial scale has remained a dream – but the United Nations Association has given it a token reality through its International Service Department, which sends volunteers to work alongside the specialists of such UN agencies as the World Health Organisation or the Food and Agriculture

Organisation. They have taken part in the literacy campaigns organised by UNESCO; worked for the refugees under the care of the UN High Commissioner or of UNRWA, the UN agency responsible for the welfare of the Arab refugees from Palestine; and they have also joined in the same kind of emergency relief work as IVS, and organised work-camps in many parts of the world which symbolise the new spirit of international coopera-tion.

Australian and New Zealand volunteers had been operating a similar scheme in Indonesia since 1952, and the same ideas were stirring elsewhere when in 1961 the Americans, under the dynamic leadership of President Kennedy, leaped with characteristic panache into the arena. None of your cautious beginnings for them, no hesitancy in high places, no need for a careful softening-up of potentially useful opinion. Instead it was the youthful President himself who seized the initiative and with a flourish and a fanfare launched the American Peace Corps. Its target was to be 5000 volunteers (within five years it had twice this number in the field) who might be of any age or sex, but must possess some skill or qualification that was needed in the under-developed world, and must undertake to serve for not less than two years. They would have behind them the authority and the resources of the American Government, which undertook to give them the local rate of pay while they worked overseas and a resettlement grant of 75 dollars for every month of their service. Congress was persuaded to set aside 30 million dollars for the first year of the scheme's operation, and Kennedy appointed as its first director Sargent Shriver, who was the President's brother-in-law and had himself gained distinction as President of the Chicago Board of Education.

It is curious now to recall the doubtful reception which the Peace Corps received, not so much in the countries where its volunteers were to serve – though there were suspicions, not unnatural ones, that its purpose would be primarily one of political infiltration – but in the United States itself. I can re-member vividly the ridicule which the idea aroused among

Americans where I was living, in the Arab world. The image of overgrown boy scouts, whose parochial habits and political naïvety would make them, and America too, a laughing-stock abroad, was a current one among critical Americans. Something of this still persists, and of course no organisation operating on such a scale, and in such a spirit of impulsive benevolence, could have failed to provide some ammunition for the critics. What was remarkable was the swiftness with which these criticisms were stifled, as the volunteers proved their value and as it became apparent that Kennedy and Shriver envisaged in the Peace Corps no latter-day children's crusade, but a thoroughly practical and workmanlike contribution to the world's development problems.

What concerns us here is the effect that the creation of the Peace Corps had on the fortunes of VSO – and that effect was considerable. To some readers it will come as a surprise to learn that the Peace Corps is younger than VSO, that indeed Shriver's first steps in organising it were influenced and to some extent guided by the experience of VSO and by the advice he sought from Alec Dickson. It is right to record this – but proper in the same breath to add that the Peace Corps, not only because of the scale of its operations but also because of its vigour and its generally professional approach to the problems of development, caused an immediate rethinking of the whole concept of voluntary service.

To begin with, it constituted for VSO from the outset what you could consider as a challenge but what came very close to being a threat. With its insistence on qualifications and on a minimum of two years' service, it promised to be to VSO what the machine-gun was to the rifle, or the rifle to the bow and arrow. Shriver might have benefited from Dickson's experience, but when he was ready to launch his craft it was not merely an enlarged version of the original prototype; it was something different in kind from VSO as it was then constituted, more of a half-way house between the voluntary agency for the provision of unqualified manpower (which VSO essentially was) and the professional organisation like FAO, able to supply – at a price – experts with high qualifications in their own fields.

74

Then again the Peace Corps, with its 30 million dollar budget and its standing as an agency of the American Government, raised the question of financial backing. Was it feasible, or desirable, to run a volunteer-sending organisation which planned to finance its operations by private subscription and by contributions from charitable trusts and foundations? Would this limit too severely its ability to expand; could it indeed function effectively without some more assured source of lasting support? The alternative was a regular government subsidy, with all the implications that this would involve for the freedom of action of VSO, its true independence, its freedom from political motivation. The problem was a complex one and it drove those who tried to solve it into some characteristically British attitudes. Conscious of the long tradition in this country of voluntary service, there were those who wanted at all costs to keep the movement free from any suggestion of government interference – and beyond this there was the strong feeling, inherent in George Edinger's original plea and in Dickson's whole approach, that the essential point of VSO was that it should escape from the human limitations of officialdom. The young volunteer was not to be a less efficient copy of the old type of colonial servant; he was to be something new and original, whose value would consist precisely in the fact that he was young and informal and able therefore to penetrate and make himself at home in an alien society in a way which was not open to anyone remotely identifiable as an 'official'.

Against this line of thinking there were those who were mistrustful of what they saw as an incorrigibly British spirit of amateurism. They saw the question of financial backing as only part of a much wider question, indeed of a whole series of interconnected questions about the purpose of VSO and the best means of achieving it, of the propriety of sending untrained enthusiasts to countries desperately in need of high-level technical advice, of the extent to which it was possible to do anything useful in this field without the impetus and the resources which only a government department could provide.

When the Peace Corps was launched, in March 1961, VSO

had ninety volunteers serving in twenty-six different countries. It had just embarked on a five-year plan, whose aim was to increase the number of volunteers to a total of 450 in 1965, and meanwhile to build up an organisation which would be able, after 1965, to put 500 volunteers into the field each year. Allowing for a certain amount of help with free passages, the cost of the programme was estimated at £20,000 in 1961, rising to just under £100,000 in 1965. But those five years were to see a far greater expansion in numbers and a fundamental change of approach, which was not achieved without a good deal of heart-searching but which was inevitable, not only because of the challenge of the Peace Corps but also in the light of the progress made in the developing countries themselves. On both counts, there was a new emphasis from 1961 on qualifications; the Peace Corps undertook to provide them, and the developing countries had more need of them, as they found their feet and laid the foundations of their own new institutions.

VSO had taken the first step in this direction very early in the day. The first year's volunteers had all been boys leaving school; but in 1959, besides two girls, the contingent had included four craft apprentices, whose activities had opened up a whole new dimension for VSO. These young technicians enjoyed the same advantage which the other volunteers had found was theirs, of being old enough to be taken seriously but young enough to be able to mix on roughly equal terms with those whom they went to instruct; but nobody could call them amateurs. They had particular skills to impart – and what was even better, they could adapt these skills to all sorts of uses in the often unpredictable environment of the developing countries.

Take the experience of an ex-apprentice from the Rolls-Royce factory in Derby, who went out in 1960 to a community development centre in Ethiopia. Other volunteers had already been helping at the centre, in a literacy programme for adults, and the idea was that the new volunteer should take the scheme a stage further, using his technical knowledge to show the inhabitants how to improve their own living conditions. He helped them to build new houses, laid on a water supply, wired the houses for electricity and trained Ethiopians to continue this work; but at this point he had trouble with an ulcer and was moved into Addis Ababa, to be within reach of a doctor when the rainy season made travel difficult outside the capital. There he was attached to a surgeon working for the Fund for the Disabled, who had started a workshop to make artificial limbs. The scheme was in its infancy, and the volunteer found scope for his mechanical skill in modifying and improvising appliances which he went on to produce in the workshop – with such success that VSO was asked to supply another volunteer to carry on what soon became a self-supporting programme. Since then a succession of other ex-apprentice volunteers have maintained the connection between VSO and the work of rehabilitation for the disabled in Ethiopia.

From such beginnings grew up what came to be known as the Development Section of VSO. Its activities widened rapidly to take in volunteers in the fields of agriculture and medicine; it supplied assistants to District Commissioners; it grew accustomed to requests for anything from a librarian to an umbrella-maker. What was significant about it was that its expansion went hand in hand with an increase in knowledge about the precise needs of the developing countries. As these countries approached independence, the more obvious problems that would confront them were considered, but very little thought was given, certainly before 1960, to the particular shortage of manpower and technical experience that they would face. The withdrawal of the colonial power meant often that all kinds of unforeseen gaps appeared, at all levels, in the structure of administrative and economic life – and this occurred just when the new society was most eager to expand and to demonstrate that independence meant a widening of opportunities, not a contraction. The problem, of course, was one which called for solutions at government level; but in supplying some of the smaller cogs without which the whole machine of development would remain ineffectual, there was a place for the volunteer with particular experience or skill who could help to keep the bigger wheels turning.

But it was in the field of education that VSO found its greatest opportunity. Education was fundamental to the whole business of development, which in essence meant the process of so remodelling backward societies that they would be able to hold their own in the modern world. A society without education was as helpless as an army without weapons; no amount of patriotic enthusiasm, no heady slogans, could overcome this shortcoming – and all along the line, as independence approached or was achieved, the developing countries found their energies frustrated, their ambitions thwarted, by this basic handicap. There was the need, first of all, to train the men and women in whose hands would lie the destinies of these new nations, those who, in the administration, in commerce, in the professions, in industry, would have a vital role in the creation of a new society. But this was not all, for the best leadership could achieve little if at a lower level its decisions ran aground on the shoals of ignorance – if a local official misinterpreted the orders of his superiors, a foreman could not understand the directions for assembling a piece of equipment, or a tractor driver put the petrol into the hole marked 'OIL'. Without education, in short, technical assistance – or indeed any assistance at all – was seed scattered on stony ground; for want of education, whole communities stood condemned to a life which the prospect of independence might brighten but could not materially improve.

Again this was a matter for concerted action at the highest level, and the early 'sixties saw a variety of national and international schemes to combat illiteracy, to promote educational exchanges, to supply teachers and build up research institutes. They achieved a lot, but they faced always the contrast between the rapidly expanding demand and the limited supply: the supply, not only of material resources, but also, and above all, of manpower. New schools were springing up all over Africa and Asia, new universities were being created, and sometimes their equipment and facilities were as modern as any in the world. The new generations were crowding into them, hungry for the knowledge and the techniques which would qualify them as modern men.

The problem, and it was one which became more and not less acute as time passed, was to find the teachers, to fill the gaps in a front that lengthened daily and which ran right through the under-developed world.

In its early days, VSO gained acceptance as one of the minor auxiliaries in this campaign. Its volunteers went to remote places where some individual known to VSO needed help and where the need, as a rule, was not so much for qualifications as for qualities: willingness and adaptability, certainly; endurance, sometimes; a sense of humour, always – and the indefinable strength that springs from a sense of purpose. They might not always be people whom the world would pick out as remarkable, like the girl from a Yorkshire grammar school, of whom someone remarked doubtfully after her interview that 'she doesn't look over-*strong*' but who fulfilled her headmaster's promise that she was 'a girl of spirit and determination' by taking over, within a few weeks of her arrival (and without apparent surprise), as headmistress of a school of 250 pupils in the Solomon Islands. That was in 1960, and it was the archetypal VSO situation, ideal both in the value of the volunteer to the project – a mission school which would otherwise have had to turn away pupils – and in the way it extended the volunteer herself, revealing in her aptitudes of which even she was probably unaware. There were many such situations, in the Falkland Islands, in Labrador, in Swaziland, where schools teetering on the brink of insolvency or threatened with extinction for lack of a teacher made eager use of an 'unqualified' volunteer – where 'qualifications' had little significance beside a willingness to tackle whatever came to hand.

As VSO grew, however, and as it became inevitably harder to handpick such projects for the growing number of volunteers, there had to be some rethinking – and it was just at this stage in the evolution of VSO that the Peace Corps came on the scene, raising related questions and in particular opening up a lively debate around this topic of qualifications. Putting it crudely, the Peace Corps seemed likely to flood the market with its thousands of volunteers, each with a college degree or some equivalent qualification in his special field. Would there still be a place for the school-leaver with a couple of 'A' levels and not a lot more that you could set down on paper (however useful you knew he could be in Sarawak or Sierra Leone)? Was there not an element of arrogance in the suggestion that because he was English he had no need of further qualifications? Ought VSO, in short, to modify its original intention and move into the field of graduate recruiting; and if so, must this be at the expense of the school-leaver scheme, or could the two be combined in a single operation whose scope would be much wider and which would be more obviously a part of Britain's contribution to the world-wide development crusade of the 'sixties?

In retrospect it seems plain enough what was the right answer. The concept of VSO was the product of two converging lines of thought: the desire to provide opportunities for enterprising young Englishmen, and the consciousness that the developing countries badly needed help in training for citizenship. If one of these had to take precedence, it could only be the second, since without such help the developing countries would be unable to fight their way into the main stream of human progress, whereas for the young Englishman VSO offered only one of various avenues of self-fulfilment.

At the time, the issue seemed less straightforward and among those who had fought so strenuously to bring VSO to life there were strong reservations about a change of emphasis which was bound to alter the organisation's character in more ways than one. What weakened their stand was the growing awareness, in those days of the 'development decade', of the tremendously varied needs of the developing countries for practical help in building up their new societies. Some of these needs, as VSO had discovered, could be met by intelligent school-leavers working under the supervision of more experienced men. But the range of opportunities for this category of volunteer was bound to remain limited and must exclude many openings where some professional qualification was necessary. For VSO deliberately to restrict its

14
Cadet volunteer
with Tibetan children at a
Save The Children Fund
Home in India

15. A volunteer working in a game park in Tanzania

16
Medical volunteer
with patients in Kenya

17. An open-air school in Zambia

activities to the field of unqualified and avowedly non-professional help would be against the trend of the times and would suggest plainly that its interest lay in providing a 'challenge' for the youth of this country rather than in going all out to offer the kind of help that was really needed. The advent of the Peace Corps made it more than ever unrealistic to think in these restricted terms.

What carried the day was the interest of the British Government in backing a scheme for graduate volunteers. As we have seen, the government had at first been sceptical about the whole idea of sending out volunteers; once the scheme was on its feet, the Colonial Office had shown interest and in 1959 had provided a grant of £9000. After that, despite various approaches, the government declined to commit itself to any form of permanent support, until the formation of the Peace Corps. Then the pressure began to build up as people began to ask why Britain had no comparable scheme in action; and went on, when they found that Britain had in fact been first in the field, to ask why VSO had received so little support from the government. Asked in the House of Commons what the government proposed to do about it, the Under-Secretary for the Colonies replied on March 21st, 1961, that Her Majesty's Government was 'always prepared to consider further assistance to organisations of this kind', adding that such assistance would depend 'on the nature of such requests for help as may be received'.

In the cautiously grey phraseology of Whitehall this meant that if VSO could show that there was a demand for its services, the government was ready to give it some backing. Well, it was not difficult to show that the demand existed; in particular, anywhere where volunteers had already served there were requests for more of them, and the target of 100 volunteers which VSO had originally set for 1961 was gradually raised until a total of 176 were eventually dispatched overseas, just twice as many as in 1960. But it was even more obvious that if the Peace Corps could think from the start in terms of 5000 volunteers, VSO could afford to raise its sights a good deal further – provided, first, that the money was forthcoming, and, second, that VSO could offer the overseas countries a service comparable to that of the Peace Corps. And that meant qualified volunteers.

In fact the VSO contingent for 1961 included, besides a larger number of apprentices from industry and a group of police cadets, the first sprinkling of graduates. They had slipped in, as it were, accidentally and they served on the same terms as the other volunteers, but they represented the thin end of what was to become a substantial wedge. Before the end of the year VSO had mounted a pilot scheme, which was largely administered by staff lent by the British Council, to send thirty-six university graduates to teach in West Africa. A few months later a committee was formed under the chairmanship of the late Sir John Lockwood, to coordinate the work of VSO and other voluntary societies (principally IVS and UNA) and to work out a comprehensive scheme of graduate voluntary service, for which the government undertook to provide financial support.

So the die was cast and VSO took – not without a great deal of individual heart-searching – an important new turning. It involved some radical changes in matters of administration and outlook, since the new-style VSO would have to function in a different way and on a different scale from the prototype. To improvise the original scheme and to maintain its impetus through the first formative years had required special qualities of energy and enthusiasm in which Alec Dickson had excelled.[1] To expand and adapt it, and to give it an administrative coherence and a more professional approach, required other qualities and less individualistic methods. For Dickson and VSO this was to be the parting of the ways, and while Dickson went on to exercise his particular gifts in the organisation of a similar scheme for voluntary service to the community at home, the deputy director, E. R. Chadwick, held the organisation together and maintained its momentum until a new director was appointed. This was Douglas Whiting, under whom VSO faced an exciting phase of expansion. From that modest beginning in 1962, the programme for graduate and

[1] And which have since been recognised by the award of the CBE.

82

qualified volunteers grew rapidly, so that within four years there were nearly a thousand of these serving all over Africa and Asia, in the West Indies and in parts of South America. Nor had the change in emphasis to qualified volunteers brought any weakening of the programme for school-leavers; indeed, as will be seen, the two were found to be in important respects complementary to each other. As the numbers of both increased it was inevitable that it should become harder to maintain the personal touch which had been such a striking characteristic of the 'Dickson era' of VSO.[1] But his successors tried hard to combine this with the more professional approach which was now required of them. Above all – for this was at the heart of Dickson's early success – they sought to maintain the standard of selection which had given VSO its initial success and on which, in the last resort, its future must depend.

[1] For a vivid picture of the Dickson era see Mora Dickson's *A World Elsewhere*.

Chapter 6

Selection and Training

It is an engaging paradox of the electronic age that in it the quality of the human element becomes more important than ever. The most elaborate machinery, the most sophisticated weapons, the most complex scientific equipment are a waste of money, an irrelevance, without the skilled manpower to operate them. If this is true of an industry or an army, it has the closest possible bearing on an organisation like VSO. No amount of effort that can go into improving its machinery, no degree of administrative efficiency – and certainly no amount of money – can achieve anything unless they serve the central purpose of selecting the right individuals and equipping them for the business in hand. VSO, in short, must stand or fall by the quality of its volunteers, and so by the effectiveness of its selection procedure. Nothing in its cycle of operations is more important than this.

Selection is not at the best of times an easy matter. Like any kind of examination, it depends in part on the interpretation of evidence which is incomplete and often imperfectly presented. It demands an understanding of psychology and an element of intuition. It is harder than ever among young people, whose aptitudes and abilities are still a matter of promise rather than of fulfilment and whose lack of self-knowledge may throw all sorts of red herrings across the trail. It is hardest of all where the individual must be selected initially, not to fill a specific and precise post, but on the basis of a combination of qualities and

84

attainments which would fit him for one of a number of different openings. And that is the situation that faces VSO.

In the early days, though only by unremitting effort, Alec Dickson and his colleagues had been able to hand pick an individual to suit a particular job. Each posting was, so to speak, tailor-made. As the numbers increased, and the requests for volunteers, this became more difficult. Faced presently with the task of recruiting several hundred volunteers every year, and anxious at all costs to retain the personal touch, VSO found the solution in breaking the selection process down into two stages. In the first stage, candidates go before a selection board and the successful ones pass into a reservoir made up of those with the right general characteristics and qualities and possessing appropriate qualifications in their own fields. From this reservoir can then be selected, in the second stage, the individual who seems best adapted to the requirements of a particular post.

It is an effective system because the market for volunteers is a fluid one, requiring flexibility on the part of VSO – and often of the volunteer himself. In fact the market is more than fluid; it is often, and for a variety of reasons, unpredictable; and the volunteer who has been chosen as much on the basis of his general aptitude as of his particular qualifications will be better able to adapt himself to the unexpected.

Consider the case of a boy who applied to VSO, with a very good reference from the headmaster of a grammar school in Lincolnshire, in the autumn of 1962. He was head boy of the school, ran a youth club with a strong emphasis on outdoor activities, and was hoping to take a course in youth leadership with the eventual aim of working in an approved school. VSO gladly accepted him as a likely candidate for youth work and offered him to Uganda, where the Ministry of Community Development had asked for two volunteers to undertake precisely this kind of work. An approved school was being built, but it was not ready when the volunteer left for Uganda in September 1963 and he was attached for the time being to a government department set up to deal with the problem of refugees arriving

85

in Uganda from neighbouring Ruanda. In this small central African territory civil war between rival tribes had led to large-scale massacres and towards the end of 1963 a growing stream of refugees poured over the border into the Western province of Uganda. Communications between this area and Kampala were difficult, and before the end of the year the volunteer (he was 19) found himself in charge of a reception camp which was receiving 250 refugees a week. They had to be fed and housed, and provided with the medical care of which many of them were in urgent need. As time went on they had to be encouraged to plant crops and reorganised into a living community, with hope and purpose for something more than mere survival. With all this the volunteer – 40 miles from the nearest town, by a road negotiable only in a Land Rover – somehow coped, learning in the process, as he wrote, 'the full extent, beauty, harshness and happiness of life'. Before taking over the post, he added:

'I was not sure whether refugee work was best for me, since I really enjoy teaching. But now every morning I see 500 children waving and grinning, who have no clothes or soap, never mind a school, and I realise that this is a greater challenge which in the end will be more enjoyable and produce (I hope) a better result.'[1]

That was an extreme case of the volunteer who undertakes one job and presently finds himself doing a totally different one. In a less striking way (and in less dramatic circumstances) many others have been called upon to adapt themselves to working at a job, or in conditions, quite different from those which they had expected. VSO tries to prevent this kind of uncertainty, but it cannot anticipate political developments which may uproot a volunteer, or the changes in the staffing position of a school or a

[1] By the time Godfrey left Uganda in September 1964 the settlement of which he was in charge at Kahunge contained 21,000 refugees. A senior official of the Ministry of Planning & Community Development wrote of him that he 'showed great devotion for his work and displayed tireless energy in helping refugees to rehabilitate themselves . . . he is never upset or downcast, no matter what the circumstances are, and he is a man of high principles. He has done a very fine job at Kahunge.'

department of education which can mean that a volunteer is transferred at short notice from one school to a quite different one, or from purely teaching duties to the supervision of sports or to youth work. Nor would it wish to be too rigid in its classifications or to insist that a volunteer delegated to do one kind of work should do that and no other. On the contrary, flexibility is and must be a part of its scheme of things, and the solution lies in trying to ensure that every volunteer, besides being equipped to do one job and do it well, will have the kind of general know-how – and of course the willingness – to try his hand at anything else that comes along.

As far as the selection process is concerned this means that in the first of the two stages I have described it is necessary for the selectors not only to explore carefully the area in which a candidate claims to be qualified, but also to have clearly in mind the general principles on which VSO operates; to understand, that is to say, just what it means to be a volunteer.

This may seem obvious enough – and yet it is not. For instance, there may be two teachers (there very often are) at the same school in a developing country, one of whom is a contract teacher while the other is a volunteer. They may do precisely the same work, and they may even share their living quarters. On paper, and more likely in the eyes of their colleagues on the staff, there is no difference between them, apart from the fact (which probably no one else realises) that one of them is paid a good deal less than the other. But there is a difference, even though it may not make itself felt anywhere but in the mind of the volunteer. The difference is that while the contract teacher has certain fixed obligations, to teach a certain subject for so many hours and perhaps to perform certain other specific duties, the volunteer has an open-ended commitment. He is there to help in whatever way he can, and if that involves spending his afternoons levelling a sports field and his evenings organising the school play or running the debating society or trying his hand at an art class, why, he's not likely to complain. For the characteristic of the volunteer – and of course it may apply also to the contract teacher, but the point is that it

87

does not necessarily – is that he wants to become involved in whatever is going on around him, to touch at as many points as possible the life of the community he has gone to serve.

This is implicit in the idea of service – but there is more to it than that. If it sounds, as I have set it down, uncomfortably idealistic, there will be plenty of volunteers to bring it down to earth, to point out that what looks on paper like self-sacrifice is in practice what you might call enlightened self-interest. Take one volunteer who went to teach in a 'bush' town of Northern Nigeria. The project, he agreed, would not be everyone's cup of tea. There was practically no social life and the nearest large town was a hundred miles away – but John found this an advantage:

'There is really very little to distract one out here and so there's nothing for it but to get on with the job. Certainly this is no ordinary teaching job; facilities for sport and practical work are minimal, so anything achieved certainly gives no little satisfaction. I can understand the Nigerian view of this as an isolated place that one is only too pleased to leave – but for the volunteer with his different ideas, I think the posting is excellent.'

Remarking that he found it 'difficult to imagine how I could have spent a more rewarding year', he listed three factors as the basis of his sense of satisfaction. The school was newly established, with very few facilities of any kind; it suffered from an acute shortage of teachers; and the atmosphere was extremely friendly. All these were accentuated by the school's remoteness, and it was this remoteness which forced on him a complete identification with a small Nigerian community and led him to sum up his experience as 'a year away from it *all* and consequently an ideal posting'.

This, of course, would not be every volunteer's conclusion in the same circumstances, but it illustrates the point about 'enlightened self-interest'. The volunteer, every volunteer, has undertaken to serve; but behind that undertaking lies in most cases a mixed bag of motives, a compound of idealism and the search for adventure, of the desire to be useful and the proper instinct of youth to stick its nose into the affairs of the rest of the world. It is the job of the selection board to ensure that the mixture is a judicious one, that the extremes of selfishness and of the kind of self-abnegation that borders on fanaticism have been eliminated. It is then up to VSO to make the best use of what remains.

In the light of all this, the selector's task – such a vital one to the proper functioning of VSO – begins to look alarmingly complex. Complex it is, and exacting; but one can strip it down to its essentials by recalling the two underlying principles on which the selection of volunteers should be based. They should be people qualified to carry out a specific and practical task, whether in teaching, medicine, agriculture or any other field of specialised activity; and they should be individuals who, in doing this, will also be able to *communicate*, to make friends, to establish between separate and sometimes antagonistic cultures the kind of contact that can lead to understanding. All else, and it may be much, is secondary. Given the right environment, a volunteer may also have the opportunity to promote new ideas, to undermine obsolete and restrictive social practices and to widen horizons artificially limited by ignorance or prejudice – but this kind of contribution will most often be incidental, almost accidental; certainly it should be the result of generally unconscious example, rather than of deliberate and didactic intention. It is made plain to the volunteer that he or she goes, not as a crusader, still less as a social revolutionary, and least of all as a representative or advocate of some British or Western 'way of life', but as an assistant, to work within an established framework and for objectives already formulated by the local authority which the volunteer undertakes to serve.

A VSO selection board consists normally of four people: a chairman, two board members and a secretary. The secretary will be a member of the staff of VSO, whose function is to keep the board informed about openings in the field of activity for which candidates are being interviewed and to record the findings and recommendations of the board. The chairman and his two colleagues may include a senior member of the staff of VSO, but normally they are drawn from the widest possible cross-section of people in public life and themselves serve as 'volunteers' at this crucial stage of VSO's operations. Around a hard core of regular chairmen, whose experience of VSO is the fruit of years of close interest and association, a panel of selectors has been built up on whose services VSO calls as often as they feel able to offer them: maybe once a fortnight, once a month, or at the irregular intervals dictated by other commitments. They include people with experience of every field in which VSO is active, and it is on the basis of their judgment of a candidate's attainments and qualities that the initial selection is made. The board's decision is final, except that the Director of VSO reserves the right to overrule it in the light of information not available to the board which may emerge later. Once the board has accepted a candidate, he or she is virtually assured of a posting overseas; it is then for the staff of VSO to examine the volunteer's particular qualifications and aptitudes and to match these as closely as possible to the requirements of a specific project.

I have set down this outline with somewhat formal precision (at the risk, I realise, of alienating the reader) because it is right that the potential volunteer should know how his case will be handled. An imaginary example may give a better idea of how a selection board works. The members will have received, some days in advance, copies of the papers of the eight or nine candidates who will come before them during the day. These papers consist of a detailed and searching questionnaire, designed to present as full a picture of the candidate's personality and achievements as can reasonably be expected to appear on paper, and of references, within the framework also of specific questions, from people able to speak with authority about the candidate from various angles. At least one member of the board, and probably more, will be experienced – as a headmaster or headmistress, an agriculturalist, a hospital matron, and so on – in the branch of work in which the candidate has offered to serve. From a study of the candidate's papers, the board has in advance some idea (occasionally an erroneous one, and very often, of course, an incomplete one, which emphasises the difficulty of committing a personality to paper) of what to expect when Miss A. is shown in.

Miss A., reading for an arts degree at a northern university (and likely, says her tutor, to get a lower second in Modern History), wants to serve as a graduate teacher, preferably – says her application form – in Ghana. She is shy, and the chairman has to ask her to speak up, but the shyness disappears when she is asked 'Why Ghana?' and answers that she has a Ghanaian friend at the university, whom she finds gay and sympathetic and from whom she has gained some idea of the difficulties of finding adequate staff for schools in the bush. Has she also formed an idea of what it would be like to spend a year in one of those schools? It seems she has and is not perturbed by the idea of loneliness; she has two or three useful hobbies, and is used to being thrown on her own resources, as her father is dead and her mother has married again. The board shows interest; a disturbed family background, leading to a sense of insecurity, is one of the commonest causes of instability in a volunteer who has to face the further tensions of a radical change of environment. But Miss A., it appears, gets on well with her stepfather, and the board, tucking the thought of him away at the back of its mind, turns to an attempt to assess Miss A.'s strength as a personality. The headmistress of the grammar school she attended in the midlands recalls her, in an enthusiastic reference, as a girl of unusual pertinacity; her college tutor, on the other hand, damning her with faint praise, seems to find her colourless. Which of them is right – the headmistress who is looking back over three years, but probably had much more to do with Miss A., or the tutor who saw her last week, but whose contacts with her may be only formal and occasional?

She doesn't look a ball of fire, the chairman is thinking, until a casual question about how she occupies her time during the vacations reveals that Miss A. has worked for the last two summers in the infirmary of a mental hospital and that during the winter she arranged a programme of play-reading for the patients. Her shyness returns as she describes this, but the board is warming to her and she recovers her confidence when asked to expand on her motives in applying to VSO. In her application form she has written: 'I know of the need for teachers overseas. By joining VSO I believe I could be of some use and at the same time gain valuable experience.' A fair mixture, the board agrees – but does Miss A. feel confident that she can teach? Confident, no, she admits candidly; but it is what she has always intended to do and she is eager to try. No, she has no experience of teaching, except that in her last year at school the sixth-form girls were sometimes put in charge of other classes and this she thoroughly enjoyed. . . .

And so, for half an hour, it goes on: an average interview, with an average candidate. When she goes out again, the board members are not long in agreeing. Each of them has a reservation, one as to her health, which has been briefly touched on but will have to be formally vouched for in a certificate from her doctor before her acceptance can be confirmed; one as to that shyness and the handicap it might represent in a teacher (but a head-mistress on the board comes down strongly in her favour); while the chairman, acting as devil's advocate, wants to be convinced that for Miss A., VSO is not a way of escape, perhaps from her domestic environment, perhaps from a world in which she does not shine as she once did at school. On examination, this idea (one for which the chairman's experience has put him on the look-out) is seen to rest only on the suggestion of insecurity in Miss A.'s home background, which all the members agree to be unjustified, and on the equivocal reference from Miss A.'s tutor. Weighing this against their own impression of Miss A. as a girl academically qualified and temperamentally suited to VSO, the board members agree to accept her, directing the board secretary (who has already done so) to make a note of her interest in Ghana and to suggest that she might be well placed, since her application form specifies that she is a practising Christian, in a mission school. And so to the next candidate.

Of all the qualities which the good selector must develop, perhaps the most difficult – and one of the most necessary – is a certain hardness of heart. Acceptance must be a positive decision

92

and the selector must fight down the impulse to say that because there is nothing substantial against a candidate he should be accepted as a volunteer. Still less can he entertain the tempting proposition that because a year or two with VSO would do a candidate so much good, or bring out his latent qualities ('make a man of him'), that candidate should be accepted. It is not just a matter for VSO of maintaining its own standards and reputation, though that is important. More important is to remember that the volunteer may go – and ideally, will go – to a situation which will test his faculties as they have not been tested before; to make the most of it he must be as far as possible unfettered by weaknesses, even though they are not of his making, that might loosen his resolve or undermine his self-confidence. And most important by far is the consideration that VSO has set out to serve the developing countries by providing them with help that is not merely willing but competent; it cannot use these countries as a proving ground, a strop to put an edge on the manhood of young Englishmen.

It is worth emphasising that idealism alone is not enough. To begin with, it is no substitute for competence; and an incompetent volunteer, however well-meaning, will be as a tinkling cymbal. Indeed, even a competent one, if his idealism be not tempered by a sense of occasion, may easily mistake his proper purpose as a volunteer. Samuel Butler remarks somewhere that 'it matters little what profession, whether of religion or irreligion, a man may make, provided only he follows it out with charitable inconsistency'. The thought is one which may set some sensitive teeth on edge; but it is a salutary one for an individual or an organisation to bear in mind, whose aim is not to impose alien ideas, but to provide practical help within an existing framework of society.

These are some of the considerations that a selection board will bear in mind. How much weight to give to each will be a matter of personal judgment, and the proportions will vary with the different types of candidate. The volunteer with a recognised qualification, a tangible skill to offer which matches a particular need, must be judged mainly on the remaining intangibles, the qualities of mind and character which distinguish the leader from the also-ran. In the case of the candidates from industry, the ex-apprentices, a useful form of pre-selection has already been carried out before the candidate reaches the selection board, by works managers or personnel officers competent to assess his technical ability. For the VSO selectors it remains to test this judgment in the light of the particular openings for which volunteers have been requested, and to question whether the candidate's personality and potential are such that he will be able to put his professional competence to good use. With a school-leaver, whose references point to abilities which can seldom, in the nature of things, be matters of established fact, the selection board must shoulder the whole task of deciding how much ability is there and how firmly it is rooted in and supported by the other ingredients of the successful volunteer.

Whatever else it is, selection cannot be an exact science. Depending as it does on human judgment, on the calculation of the sum of elements not susceptible to precise definition, it would be unreasonable to suggest, or to insist, that mistakes are not sometimes made. Paradoxically, it may be that the awareness of this will on occasion cause a selection board to err – but on the side of caution, believing that where doubt lingers it is better not to take risks whose consequences will fall on other shoulders. The judgment of the board is exercised in each individual case, not only on behalf of VSO but in the interests of some unknown school or hospital or youth centre anywhere from the Falkland Islands to Fiji – and of the candidate too, whose whole future will be affected by the outcome of the board's self-questioning. The board's decisions do not, as VSO sees it, put the stamp of success or failure on a candidate; they represent the expression of an opinion that this candidate can, while that one cannot with certainty, be fitted into the scheme of VSO's operations. It is not necessarily a question of merit, but rather of aptitude for the peculiar conditions under which a volunteer may be required to serve. Where adaptability is so vital a characteristic it may well be that the candidate whom the board is unwilling to accept has qualities (to say nothing of abilities) which will bring him or her outstanding success in another environment. To suggest a parallel, an applicant who was considered unsuitable for admission to the Franciscan order (with which, incidentally, the true volunteer must feel some kinship) might achieve notable success as a Dominican or a Jesuit, whose approach to the world is not better or worse, but merely different.

When he comes before the selection board the volunteer is, as it were, a caterpillar. Acceptance as a volunteer marks his entry into the chrysalis, where it is the responsibility of VSO to equip him with wings to fly and with the antennae which will enable him to take the measure of his future environment and to function effectively within it. More prosaically, this means that the volunteer's natural abilities and previous experience must now be focused on a specific objective, and this objective made clear in the context of the needs and the stage of development of the particular country in which the volunteer is going to serve. VSO's training programme starts from the premiss that as far as possible volunteers have been selected on the basis of aptitudes or practical attainments in a given field, whether it be education, agriculture, nursing or any of a dozen other activities. Without these, it would not now be feasible in a short time to train them; but it is possible to put an edge on these attainments or qualifications, and to give each volunteer a clear idea of how they may best be adapted to the conditions of life in one particular developing country.

This process of adaptation is not just a professional or academic one. Its social and psychological aspects may be even more important. Take the case of a girl, a graduate of London University who went out just before her 21st birthday to teach English and History in Pakistan. From the room in a mission hostel which she shared with another volunteer she looked out on a road

'full of holes and covered in a thick layer of dust and dung. There are nearly always one or two men squatting at either side to urinate, as well as beggars, peanut-wallahs and children and herds of buffaloes wandering vaguely up and down. The hostel is like a kind of oasis at the top of the road, with a fairly large garden, and the tree tops beside where I am sitting on the roof are full of eagles, crows and kites of thin paper (belonging to little boys in the nearby slums) which have got stuck. . . . At first I felt physically sick at the terrible squalor, at the sight of human life reduced to its lowest terms. I didn't want to see or smell any of it. Now I have learned to face up to it, while still feeling rather helpless. (We saw a beggar crawl across the road to die at our hostel gates, before we could do anything about it.) I have grown to love the place now but what I miss most is the glorious sense of anonymity which one has in London. . . . Everywhere one goes, especially on a bicycle, one is gaped at by endless hordes of men . . . we have learned to wear *shelwas*, the baggy trousers worn by all the women here, so that we should be less conspicuous.'

Adaptation, then, involves an adjustment both psychological and professional, and the timetable of VSO's operations imposes narrow limits within which to attempt this. The vast majority of volunteers, when they come before selection boards, are still in their final term at school, university or training college. They only become available to VSO when their final examinations are behind them, in July or August, and by September most of them must be in position overseas to undertake their new tasks. Into a period of some eight weeks has to be compressed the greater part of a programme of briefing courses, with a number of additional courses for specialist training, which will equip getting on for 1500 volunteers to work at different occupations in more than fifty countries.

The basic element in this variegated programme is the one-week course which every volunteer attends and which, apart from anything else, serves the subsidiary but not unimportant purpose of incorporating the individual into the body of VSO as a whole. There is no element here of regimentation; indeed, the emphasis, if anything, is the other way and neither VSO nor the volunteers have any wish to stamp a pattern on an organisation which functions best as the expression of responsible individualism. But there is a value in bringing together the volunteers from varied backgrounds who are going now to the same place to do the same thing. At the briefing course, whatever they learn from their instructors, they learn much from each other. If they have anxieties about what lies ahead, it is reassuring to find that these are not peculiar to themselves; and with whatever variations of a common purpose they have embarked on the life of the volunteer, they are likely by the end of the course to feel the sense of that purpose sharpened and made more coherent.

This apart, VSO's briefing courses have two main objectives: to give the volunteers background knowledge of the country in which they are to serve; and to advise them on how to make the best use of the talents they possess and on the basis of which they have been selected. A course for graduate volunteers going, say, to India to work as teachers will include lectures on Indian history, geography and political organisation; on the Indian educational system; on teaching methods in general and the teaching of English in particular, with which the majority of the volunteers will be concerned; on first aid, health and hygiene in a tropical climate. The volunteers will have received, as soon as their postings have been decided, a reading-list of books about India, and at the course they will have an opportunity to meet Indians, to see films about India and – perhaps the most useful element of all in the courses and certainly one of the most appreciated – to listen to returned volunteers who have worked in India and who alone can communicate in the volunteer's own terms the precise problems and satisfactions of working in the Indian environment. Finally, they will hear from the Director of VSO or one of his senior colleagues an explanation of what the aim is behind all this, what it is that the volunteers are being asked to do, and why, and how it may best be achieved within the framework of VSO's special terms of reference.

The terms of reference are important, for nobody would pretend that a week spent in this way could turn the brightest young graduate into a polished student of Indian affairs, or into

G   97

an experienced teacher. What it can do, given the interest and enthusiasm on which VSO must rely, is first, prepare the volunteers for the Indian experience, and second, provide them with the assurance that their own capital of learning or acquired skill, modest as it may be, can be put to effective use in the situation that will confront them. The first demands a sympathetic effort of the imagination, the kind of effort which comes easily to youth, provided only that the necessity for it is clearly presented; while the second involves a nice blend of humility and self-confidence which – however often VSO may fail to achieve it – is the hallmark of the ideal volunteer.

Confidence, of course, can only be justified by the ability to produce results, and since in this respect almost all volunteers lack the assurance of past experience, the least that VSO can do is to provide them with as great a measure of theoretical competence as possible. For some categories of volunteers, the apprentices from industry, for example, the trained nurses, or the graduates of an agricultural college, there is no problem here, since they have been accepted as volunteers after having achieved certain recognised standards of professional accomplishment. For the volunteer who is going to teach, the situation is different. A few will already have been at work as teachers for a year or two, perhaps longer – and VSO is very glad to get hold of them. Of the rest, a growing number come from the Colleges of Education (the former Teacher Training Colleges), where they will have experienced at least the periods of teaching practice which form part of the training for a certificated teacher. But the majority will be university graduates, with no formal qualification as teachers beyond their first degrees; and to these must be added the school-leavers, with no formal qualification at all. For all these, ideally, VSO would like to provide something more concrete in the way of training than two or three lectures at the standard briefing course, and in recent years courses in the teaching of English as a foreign language have been prominent in the second element of VSO's training programme. This comprises specialist courses in a number of fields, which volunteers attend in addition to the

98

basic briefing courses and which are complementary to these.

Apart from the teaching of English and teaching techniques (for both arts and science graduates without teaching experience), these specialist courses provide instruction in foreign languages and in Tropical Agriculture, Forestry, Tropical Medicine and Technical Instruction. The last of these, organised through the Ministry of Labour, is for ex-apprentices who will be teaching their own technical skills. For the 1968 contingent of volunteers VSO planned a total of 27 of these specialist courses, in addition to the 16 standard briefing courses attended by all volunteers, whatever their previous attainments or qualifications.

The question of language training is one to which VSO has not yet found a satisfactory answer. There is no doubt in anyone's mind that a volunteer going to Pakistan or Ethiopia, even if his function is to be the teaching of English to children who already have a grounding in the language, will be incomparably better off if he can speak the local language. Apart from the help it will give him in his primary role as a teacher, or as any other kind of volunteer, it may make all the difference to his chances of achieving at all the secondary purpose of making real contact with the people around him. Its usefulness will vary from country to country, and within each country, and according to the type of work he is doing. Whatever else, it will open to him windows of experience and understanding which can only benefit him and make him potentially a more effective volunteer.

So much is incontestable, but so far no one has devised a way of providing this training, within the time available and at a cost which is not disproportionate. In a small way VSO has experimented with courses in Swahili, Malay and Chinyanga (the language spoken in the southern part of Malawi) and less ambitiously in French and Spanish for volunteers going to territories where one or other is the lingua franca in the way that English is in many parts of Africa and India. It has also arranged for volunteers to attend courses in Swahili after their arrival in East Africa, and this is a promising development, although the time factor remains an uncomfortable one. These attempts represent an interim approach to the problem, for which there may be an eventual solution in the context of the recent development of language laboratories and computerised learning. It will never be vital for all volunteers to learn a local language, since many will always go to places and situations where they can communicate freely in English; and while the projects to which volunteers are attached can often be changed, as we have seen, by unpredictable factors, it might not be wise to spend a lot of time and money on learning a language which might prove useless to a volunteer diverted at the last moment into a different tribal area. But in general terms there is no question that language training would heighten the effectiveness of most volunteers, whatever they are doing and wherever they are serving.

The problem is connected to other questions which will be treated later, and in particular to the length of time for which volunteers are to serve.[1] So long as the standard term of service was twelve months, it was out of the question to devote to language training any period long enough to make that training effective. The growing emphasis on two-year service (the minimum term for volunteers from most other countries) takes the sting out of this objection but cannot dispose of it until *all* volunteers serve for two years, or at least enough of those going to a single country to make a substantial scheme of language training worth while. But VSO has solid reasons for refusing so far to insist on a minimum of two years, and it is not necessarily logical to suggest that because the Peace Corps or the German volunteer agency does (and provides language training as well) VSO ought to do the same. In many territories of the Commonwealth, where the English language and English teaching methods have never been superseded, German and even to some extent American volunteers face problems which are much less troublesome to their English counterparts.

Reverting to training in its broader aspects, there is a third element in VSO's training programme which has proved of great value in reinforcing the groundwork laid at the regular briefing

[1] See Chapter 12.

courses and the further specialist training provided for many volunteers in their chosen fields. This again will be dealt with in a later chapter[1] but briefly it consists of what may be called adaptation courses, held in the country where the volunteers are serving. Especially valuable to the teaching volunteer, these courses concentrate on special factors in the local environment which can affect the work the volunteers are doing. The implications of African nationalism, or of the segregation of women in Moslem society, are more easily comprehended in the environment of which they form an essential part than in the remote calm of an English classroom; and volunteers will more readily appreciate the special problems of teaching in a Malaysian village once that village has begun to seem like home to them.

Selection and training – these are the two points of contact between VSO and the volunteers before they go overseas. After that, contact is not lost, certainly; but it is necessarily more tenuous. To a large extent it becomes a matter of choice for the volunteer, who may respond more willingly or less to VSO's attempts to retain the personal link. Either way, he remains 'on the strength', with a gradually swelling file and a personality that grows more distinct the more regularly he corresponds with headquarters. At most, he will receive in the course of a year a single visit from a member of the staff of VSO. But however remote his situation he is not likely to lose touch either with the organisation or with his colleagues in the field. The latter, whom he got to know at the briefing course in England, are spread about over some hundreds or thousands of square miles around him, providing a ready-made network of contacts and potential hosts. He is likely to meet them once or twice at one of the overseas courses I have mentioned; and most probably he will call in on them when he has an opportunity to travel, or find them (especially if he occupies some post which is scenically enviable) laying out their sleeping-bags in his living-room. At times, especially during the school holidays, there are mountain slopes in Africa which

---

[1] See Chapter 7.

seem to be positively crowded with volunteers, alone or in convoy, making a now almost traditional pilgrimage.

As for VSO itself, it is far away now, a presence as shadowy for the volunteer – if he or she chooses – as Whitehall was, a generation ago, to the colonial administrator in his remote imperial fastness. But there is a difference. For all its remoteness, VSO has in every territory where volunteers are working an agent, whose role is an important one both for the effectiveness of VSO's operations and for the welfare of the individual volunteer. This is the British Council, whose function as the 'overseas arm' of VSO it is now time to examine.

Chapter 7

The Overseas Arm

If the first imperative for VSO is to pick the right volunteers, the second – no less vital – is to ensure that they have something worth while to do. The one without the other will achieve nothing, and the better the volunteer the more he will resent it if the job he has been asked to do turns out to be unsatisfying or badly thought out. Nor, when that happens, will the harm be confined to the waste of a volunteer and the frustration of a young man who knows he could be spending his time better. For when the volunteers return home after their service, it is their verdict on the experience that will most influence their successors. VSO would not have expanded in the way that it has over the past ten years if the great majority of the volunteers had not come home convinced of the value of the scheme and of their own part in it.

A good 'project' is no easier to come by than a good volunteer. Indeed, of the two it is the project that is hardest to run to ground. It is not just a matter of hearing of a school or a hospital, an agricultural station or a youth centre or a new university somewhere in the developing world which needs help. That's a beginning – but then the questioning starts. Why does it need help, and how badly? Is there some special factor which prevents it from recruiting staff in the ordinary way, or is the difficulty that funds are lacking? If so, has it the financial resources to support a volunteer, who costs relatively little but still has to be fed and lodged? Above all, is there a real job to be done, and if so, what are the precise qualifications needed? And when all these questions have been answered, there remain a host of more mundane ones which need to be asked before VSO can be satisfied first, that here is a project which it can tackle and second, that it will be able to provide a volunteer to suit this particular situation. Even then it will be necessary to keep in touch with the project, to be aware of any change in its circumstances (which may be due to factors as diverse as a change of headmasters or a civil war) which might affect the position of a volunteer.

A project, in short, has first to be discovered; then it must be thoroughly investigated; if it is adopted it needs still to be supervised – and all this at a distance of some thousands of miles from VSO's London headquarters. When the volunteers were numbered in tens and were all school-leavers, this was already a problem. As they multiplied into hundreds, and engaged in every kind of activity in fifty or sixty countries, the problem became acute – and as more and more of them had specific qualifications which it was important to put to effective use, it became ever more vital to find a proper solution.

Various solutions were canvassed. So long as the number of volunteers remained manageable, it might be possible to provide the necessary supervision by means of frequent and extensive foreign tours by the staff of VSO. Even this idea would not enable the organisers of the programme to keep in really close touch with the volunteers in the field and with those who employed them; and it would be extravagant, in terms of time as well as money – and would become unworkable once the number of volunteers increased beyond a certain point. An attractive alternative was for VSO to retain permanent representatives overseas, who could devote all of their time to visiting projects in different areas, attend to the welfare of the volunteers and report back to London on any new project which might be proposed. In many respects this seemed the ideal solution – it was the one which the Peace Corps adopted – but it would be even more expensive, increasing the average cost of each volunteer by something like 25%, which was out of the question in terms of VSO's available budget. To adopt it would simply mean that the number of volunteers would have to be reduced.

The only other solution was to make use of some other organisation, or some network of individuals, who were already on the spot. To some extent this was what had happened in the very early days of VSO, when personal acquaintances of Alec Dickson had suggested openings for volunteers and had taken some measure of responsibility for supervising their placing and their welfare once they were overseas. But it seemed over-optimistic to imagine that this system could be extended to match the growing scale of VSO's operations.

After the initiation of the scheme for qualified volunteers in 1962 the expansion had been rapid. In that year 320 volunteers were sent overseas, of whom thirty-six were university graduates. In 1963 the total was 500, including 150 graduates or holders of other professional qualifications, and in 1964 the number of these qualified volunteers more than doubled so that they were providing nearly half of VSO's total contingent of 730 volunteers. And the means by which this expansion was achieved pointed the way to a solution of the problem of overseas representation.

When Dickson was launching his original scheme for school-leaver volunteers, a similar scheme had been set on foot by the British Council.[1] For four years the two ran on roughly parallel courses, until the British Council's 'cadet' scheme was merged with VSO just when VSO was preparing its venture into the graduate field. During this time the two organisations had exchanged ideas and worked to some extent in liaison with each other. The British Council had a direct interest in the teaching side of VSO's work, since one of the Council's main preoccupations was to encourage and promote the teaching of English overseas. When the structure of VSO was reorganised and strengthened in 1961, the Director-General of the British Council, Sir Paul Sinker, had joined the Council of VSO and from then on took a close interest in its workings. A year later, when the government agreed to sponsor the new scheme for graduate volunteers, the

[1] See Chapter 5.

105

British Council offered to help VSO by providing the administrative staff to see the scheme through its formative years. The graduate programme was in fact run during its first two years by a small unit working within VSO but headed by an officer of the British Council, J. R. Bunting.

During these two years the habit of cooperation developed, and it was one which had advantages both for the British Council and for VSO. The Council, under pressure to find an ever-increasing number of English teachers to work in the developing countries, was only too well aware of the growing need, and it was in a good position to spot the openings in which a volunteer could at least hold the fort. VSO, with its catchment area now extending from the secondary schools into the universities, was well placed to provide a growing number of reinforcements for the teachers recruited by the Council. The collaboration proved fruitful for both, and before VSO took over from the Council the whole administration of the graduate programme in 1964, an understanding had been reached whereby the British Council agreed to take on the responsibility of acting as VSO's 'overseas arm'. What this meant in practice was that while VSO found the volunteers and attended to all the details of selecting and training them and transporting them to their destinations, the Council would explore the openings in the developing countries, examine the projects which were submitted, and supervise the welfare of the volunteers during their term of service.

The new arrangement aroused some opposition among those who misunderstood the true nature and role of the British Council. The essence of their criticism was that the association with the British Council would endanger one of the programme's fundamental aims: to get away from the old, official pattern of colonial administration with its overtones of paternalism, and build a new pattern with a less formal basis of cooperation between equals. To the critics, the British Council was too closely associated with the old régime. Its semi-official status, its hierarchical structure, its very size, so the argument ran, made it too odd and inappropriate a bedfellow for a voluntary organisation whose lifeblood was youth, and whose nature presupposed a certain enthusiastic, even impulsive approach to life which would be out of keeping with the staid bearing of a body like the British Council. In concrete terms, their objection was that to link VSO with the Council would alter its character, subjecting the volunteers to pressures which would transform them into replicas of the old colonial servants – whose legacy in many cases might be admirable, but whose corporate image was hopelessly out of date in the new society struggling to find an identity in the developing world.

Experience soon showed that this was a short-sighted view. The fact is that the new departure did involve a change of emphasis, if not of approach – but it was a change which was logical as a reflection of VSO's growing potential in the field of development. The developing countries were crying out for qualified help; and the resources mustered under the slogan of the development decade were proving inadequate to meet the demand. There was an opportunity for VSO, as there was for the Peace Corps and for the other voluntary agencies now springing up in various parts of Europe and North America, to play a significant part in bolstering the supply; but if their part was indeed to be significant, it must not only be substantial in size but also effective in content. The effort must be directed where it was most needed and it was vital that its resources must be put to the best use. All this pointed to the provision of a widespread and competent network of overseas supervisors, locally based so that they could be properly aware of local needs, and whose status would be such that they could negotiate with assurance the pitfalls of local attitudes and reservations.

There was another aspect to the situation created by VSO's steady expansion. As the numbers climbed towards the thousand mark, and as the individual volunteers were scattered ever more widely over territories where communications were often poor and the political future uncertain, there was an obvious need for some machinery of control which could be set in motion in time of emergency – and emergency in this context could mean anything from earthquake or famine to war, tribal, civil or international. It could also mean a volunteer who developed appendicitis at an up-country settlement in Tanzania, or broke a leg in Thailand, or had to be swiftly summoned home from the Falkland Islands because of some family crisis in Britain. All these were the kind of situations which could be easily handled so long as the volunteers in a single country could be numbered on the fingers of two hands; but once there were fifty or even a hundred, in a country many times the size of Britain, it was essential that someone should assume clear-cut responsibility for them, and should be in a position to act promptly on their behalf when the occasion arose.

In all these contexts the British Council was well placed to look after VSO's interests. It was present in virtually every territory where volunteers were operating. Its representatives were in touch with government departments and were normally on friendly terms with the kind of officials with whom it would be necessary to negotiate terms of service for volunteers. In most countries it had branch offices dispersed though different regions, to which volunteers could turn for professional or personal advice and assistance. Its staff included experts in the teaching of English, with which the majority of volunteers would be directly or indirectly concerned. Above all, its officers were in a good position to assess the needs of a country, particularly in the field of education, to weigh the value of one project against another, to investigate the requests received for volunteers, to see that at any project which VSO decided to take on, the conditions existed which would allow a volunteer to function as effectively as possible.

Nobody could say with certainty, when the new arrangement was adopted at the beginning of 1964, how it would work in practice. To all it was plain that in assuming a measure of responsibility for the volunteers, the representatives of the British Council would be taking on duties which some of them might find uncongenial. It was easy for the critics to go further and to point the contrast between the traditional caricature of the British Council officer, all string quartets and Jane Austen, and the image of the clean-limbed young volunteer with whom he was now to be associated. Was not this asking oil and water to mix? And from VSO's point of view could the result be other than a process of sophistication which must weaken the original high resolve?

The answer, with few exceptions, proved quite otherwise, and events were to show how eminently valuable the new connection would prove. Nor was the Council the loser by it, since the volunteers provided for the Council's officers access to levels of indigenous society which it would have been hard for them to penetrate on their own. If there was an element of stiffness, an inherent sobriety, in the approach of the Council, association with the volunteers has certainly helped in some cases to loosen it. If a volunteer, here or there, has been startled to find himself treated by his African or Asian colleagues with the deference due to someone whom they regarded as a British Council dependant, so has the odd British Council representative experienced a not disagreeable surprise at being casually mistaken for just another volunteer.

Since the start of the partnership with the British Council, VSO's Director and his staff have travelled more extensively than before, with the objective of visiting, once a year, each main area where volunteers are at work. But during that time the number of volunteers has doubled, and the variety of their work has greatly increased, so that without the help of the British Council the amount of supervision which VSO could have provided would have been proportionately very much smaller. Not the least useful function of the Council in its role as overseas arm is the preparatory work its representatives do for these visits by VSO staff members, whose task of covering a great deal of ground in a short time is made very much easier by the advice and the practical help of the men on the spot. Having travelled widely myself as a lone newspaper correspondent, without the benefit of any helpful agency to make my appointments, see me through customs, arrange my travel bookings and hotel reservations, I can testify to the difference it makes to be able to rely on someone else for all these – and to enjoy his company into the bargain at the end of a long day.

Supervision, in the sense of keeping an eye on the volunteers at work, is a subsidiary part of the work of the overseas arm, a bonus, if you like, or a kind of insurance policy. Not many of the volunteers would like it to be more, and many would resent it, rightly feeling that they can be trusted to get on with the job without anyone looking over their shoulders. If the project has been well planned, it should look after itself, and in the great majority of cases this is what does happen. The value of the overseas arm in this context lies in its ability to intervene when things do not go as they should: to sort out the minor problems of accommodation or environment, to correct the situation when a volunteer is misemployed or under-employed (which is far more likely to upset him than if he is overworked), to arrange for the provision of transport or special equipment which may make all the difference to the effectiveness of a volunteer. If something more fundamental is amiss, if a clash of temperaments or some other unforeseen circumstance has put a square peg into a round hole, the nearest British Council representative will be able to discover the root of the trouble and, if there is no other solution, to arrange for the volunteer to be transferred elsewhere.

Health is inevitably a constant preoccupation to VSO. Apart from the responsibility to the volunteers (and to their parents) to see that their health is protected by every means that can be provided, there is the practical consideration that a sick volunteer is no use to anyone. Before they go overseas the volunteers are given detailed advice (some of them have found it almost comic in the range of its gloomy forebodings) about how to look after themselves in the unfamiliar climates which await them. They have been examined, vouched for, inoculated and instructed about everything from bilharzia to jigger fleas and the hazards of hitch-hiking. But no precautions can be infallible and if a volunteer falls seriously ill, or is involved in an accident, it is enormously reassuring to VSO to know that the overseas arm will be able to see that the best medical attention is available, to arrange

110

for the volunteer to be repatriated if that should seem necessary, or to furnish the detailed information for which parents will be impatient in such a situation.

In emergencies still more far-reaching, the value of an overseas arm as substantial and ubiquitous as the British Council is self-evident.[1] The emergency might be personal, involving some combination of pressures on a volunteer already isolated and hard-worked, whose sum might be too great for him to cope with alone and which it might be hard for him to discuss with those around him. It might involve the severe illness, perhaps the death, of a parent, and the need for the volunteer to fly home at short notice. It might – indeed it not infrequently does – centre around a girl-friend whose acceptance of his long absence weakens as time goes by, posing for him a harsh choice of loyalties. (This is a situation which VSO tries hard, and inevitably sometimes fails, to avoid.) Or again the emergency may be a quite extraneous one, the result of war or revolution which may or may not threaten the safety of the volunteer, but which either way is bound to seem infinitely menacing to his family five thousand miles away. In all these situations – and there is seldom a time when some variant of one or other of them is not raising a ground-swell of anxiety somewhere in the world – VSO has reason to be grateful to its overseas arm for reassurance, swift intercession and, where it becomes necessary, prompt and effective action. Whenever possible, this action is only taken after consultation with VSO in London; but *in extremis* the overseas arm has the authority to exercise its own initiative.

If in all these respects the British Council has proved its varied worth to VSO, its main function is much more than that of a friend and counsellor to the volunteers, or a reliable longstop in times of crisis. Involved as it is on VSO's behalf in an infinitude of administrative detail concerning itself with the health of the volunteers, their accommodation, transport, allowances, their liability to

[1] In the few territories where there are volunteer projects but where the British Council does not operate, the British Embassy or High Commission normally accepts the functions of the overseas arm for VSO.

customs charges and income tax, the textbooks they use and the equipment they need, their personal problems and their professional dissatisfactions, their distribution to their projects when they arrive in the country and their subsequent repatriation (orderly or abrupt, as the exigencies of life in the developing world may dictate) – its primary and essential task is to help VSO to direct its efforts and its resources where they will be of most use. This means, above all, help in the choice of projects to which volunteers are to be sent, and the provision of detailed information about each, on the basis of which VSO will be able to choose not just a volunteer, but as far as possible the appropriate volunteer for that particular situation.

This calls for tact as well as insight, for VSO of course can only operate (and the British Council too, for that matter) with the approval of the government of the country concerned. Almost invariably these governments are closely interested in questions of development and they naturally want to exercise some control over the functions and the distribution of the volunteers working in their territories. The extent of this control will vary: some governments, whose development plans are elaborate and precise, will be anxious to coordinate the activities of volunteers with those of existing development agencies; in other countries, the disposition of the volunteers will be more haphazard and the responsibility for seeing that they are well placed will devolve more on VSO and its overseas arm. Either way, and especially where qualified volunteers are concerned, the initiative must come from the overseas government, which suggests the projects and applies for the volunteers to fill them. The task of the British Council, acting for VSO, is to help in this process of project selection; to investigate every likely project, explain why some projects are unsuitable within VSO's terms of reference and suggest others for the government's approval; and finally to forward to VSO precise specifications of every project on the list which is finally approved.

This is a vital stage in VSO's cycle of operations and its successful negotiation depends ultimately on the thoroughness with which the overseas arm plays its part. However well projects are selected and however accurately the British Council reflects the requirements of each, there will always be a margin of error, if only because so much can change about a project during the six months or so that must elapse between the time when it is first recommended and the time when a volunteer finally arrives. Nothing can provide against the rapid alteration that may take place in the character and fortunes of a school when a strong headmaster retires; or the sudden decline that can overtake the most promising experiment in community development when it becomes the plaything of an ambitious politician, or is caught in the crossfire of tribal jealousies. From VSO's point of view the advantage of the British Council as an ally and an agent is that it is well placed to chart such variations in the local temperature and to intervene when they affect the fortunes of its volunteers.

In one other respect the overseas arm, acting this time on an initiative of its own, has reinforced VSO's machinery for placing the volunteers and seeing that they are equipped for the tasks they undertake. Within a year of accepting its new responsibilities, the British Council offered to supplement VSO's training programme by organising further short courses for the volunteers once they had arrived overseas. A first experiment in Nigeria in 1965 suggested that this could be a useful innovation. Stimulated by their first contact with their new environment, the volunteers were already alive to the nature of the challenge that confronted them. Standing literally on the threshold of a new experience, with the sights and sounds of Nigeria tickling their senses, subject already to the heady influences of climate and vegetation, and above all of the novelty and vitality of African life, their perceptions were sharpened. What had required an impossible effort of the imagination when it was presented to their attention back in England now stood sharply before their eyes, and was already on the way to becoming familiar to the receptive appetite of youth. It was as though one tried to read a map of a territory wholly unknown – and then unfolded the same map again after a first journey through the area. Landmarks had begun to take on

H   113

substance, the contours suddenly had meaning. The volunteers were on the way to feeling at home and so were able to apprehend nuances which a short time before had been indistinguishable to them.

Since then the experiment has been widely repeated, has become in fact a standard part of the pattern of volunteer training. Distance and the problem of communications present obstacles which cannot everywhere be overcome, but wherever possible courses of this kind have been arranged and are held either when the volunteers first arrive or – and this seems to give the best results – when the experience of the first weeks or months has prepared their minds, like soil under the plough, for the seeds of closer understanding. Sometimes these courses can be organised in conjunction with other voluntary agencies, bringing together volunteers from Britain and those from America, Canada and other countries – and this gives them an additional point since, with minor variations, all are pursuing the same objectives.

Project selection, help in emergencies, the provision of an administrative framework for the overseas part of VSO's work, an addition to the training programme – these are the main contributions of the British Council to a partnership which has grown steadily more confident and effective since it was started in 1964. On points of administrative detail it has been gradually codified in a book of advice issued by the Director of VSO (to whom, in their role as members of the overseas arm, British Council representatives are responsible); and every summer, when the British Council holds a conference in Britain at which its overseas representatives can exchange views, one session is set aside for a discussion of the Council's part in VSO's affairs, with members of the VSO staff taking part. These exchanges are helpful to both sides, providing a clearing-house at which misunderstandings can be examined and new suggestions entertained – but essentially the partnership remains as informal and pragmatic as the British constitution. Perhaps the key to its success is the fact that where the developing countries are concerned the aims of the British Council and of VSO are very similar. The collaboration between them owed much to the personal interest of Sir Paul Sinker. On his retirement as Director-General of the British Council in 1968, Sir Paul mentioned as one of the memorable features of his term of office the extension of the links between the Council and VSO. Each sets out to give practical assistance where it is asked for; and, in doing this, each tries to broaden the areas of contact between the new generations in Britain and in the rest of the world. In this sense, and with all their differences, they are natural allies.

Chapter 8

Volunteers in Education

We are familiar enough these days with the sad proposition that half the world goes hungry. There is much less emphasis on the less dramatic fact (and of course the two are related) that much of the world is starved of education. It is this as much as anything that has provided the opportunity for VSO, and two-thirds of the volunteers it sends abroad go to teaching posts, while many of the others, though they may be engaged in practical work of one kind or another, serve also as instructors in their own particular fields.

There are few generalisations which one can risk about the teaching side of VSO's work. It embraces university projects and primary schools, with every imaginable gradation between the two, as well as work in approved schools and specialised institutions of various kinds. It provides openings for the trained teacher, the university graduate and the school-leaver, each of whom can offer a contribution acceptable at some level somewhere in the world. There is in this statement neither patronage nor wishful thinking; it is simply the reflection of an unpalatable fact, on which we must dwell for a moment.

Approximately one half of the world's population lives in what we call the developing countries.[1] There is no hard and fast dividing line between the developing and the developed – a better term might be the industrialised countries – but certain broad characteristics distinguish those whom the economists or the

---

[1] This excludes China, which accounts for almost a half of the remainder.

sociologists would place in one category or the other. The developing countries, many of whom have been independent for less than a decade, vary in all sorts of ways among themselves, but in general they are characterised by a low standard of living and a high birth rate. These two interact and combine to retard development of every kind, and most of the efforts that have been made to bring about an improvement, to narrow the gap between the poor nations and the rich, have foundered on the reefs of ignorance, on the absence at every level of a sufficient number of men and women capable of manipulating the instruments of a modern state. To throw off this limitation is the prime need of the developing countries.

To achieve this, however, is far from easy. Even if it were possible swiftly to build the schools and the higher institutes which are needed, and to equip them with the necessary facilities, the problem would remain of finding qualified teachers; and these are not available among populations themselves largely illiterate. Reliable statistics are hard to come by, but it has been uncertainly calculated that throughout the developing countries as a whole the adult illiteracy rate is something like 75%; in other words, that three adults out of four are unable to read or write. Generally speaking, the younger generation is better off – but there are still countries where only one child in ten has the opportunity of going to a secondary school, and few developing countries where this privilege is open to even one half of the children of school age. As for higher education, the opportunities are of course infinitely more restricted and the obstacles more variegated. Even in a country with a rapidly expanding economy, like Colombia, or one with great natural resources, like Saudi Arabia, the peasant or the herdsman has as little chance of attending a university as of flying to the moon – perhaps less, the way things are going.[1] The obstacles are not purely material; behind the shortages and the inadequacies lie equally formidable barriers of

[1] This is not as flippant as it sounds. There are millions of people in the world to whom the jet airliner is a familiar means of transport but who have never ridden in a train, or even seen one.

117

convention and prejudice, which limit as ruthlessly as sheer poverty the horizons of the dispossessed.

The only safe generalisation then is that the need for a huge expansion of educational opportunities exists throughout the developing world, that it is urgent and acute – and that without it much of the effort that is lavished on development schemes of every kind is bound to be sterile and unproductive. In this context, and at every level of this pattern of need, there is clearly a wide scope for the volunteer, both as the straightforward recruit in an educational task force and with the more subtle (and no less necessary) function, for which his very youth may especially qualify him, of changing people's attitudes to education and to the world about them.

'At every level' – this is the keynote of VSO's work in the field of education, and it raises constant questions about the aim in view and the right way to achieve it. As things stand, the volunteers are dispersed, not haphazardly but with a certain waywardness (as VSO is the first to acknowledge) over much of the globe and in a variety of institutions, from the humblest of mission schools to the most resplendent of new universities. Some of them have been startled, when they arrived, to find themselves surrounded by equipment superior to anything they had known in their own schooldays in Britain. Others have been posted to schools which they had first to lend a hand with building, before they could settle down to teach in them. The objective, one which requires constant revision and readjustment on the part of VSO, is to place them where they are most needed and best able to make themselves useful – and if that sounds easy, it is not meant to. The needs are so various, and the factors which make for a successful 'project' so intangible (depending in the last resort on the individual human reaction to a given set of circumstances) that no final and immutable pattern can ever be devised. The most that can be hoped for is that the volunteers be deployed where each of them can feel conscious of a need and able in some degree to meet it.

Sometimes the need is obvious enough, as when a girl volunteer in the Solomon Islands writes that 'if I had not arrived half the school would have been sent home for lack of staff'; or in the case of the school in Montserrat, the only secondary school in this West Indian island, whose science department would have had to close down without the two volunteers dispatched to keep it going. To the right sort of volunteer there is a special stimulus in the kind of situation one graduate reported from a 'bush' school in Northern Nigeria:

'This term I am having to earn my keep', he wrote, since 'over the holiday we lost half our members of staff due to the Government take-over from the Native Authority. With the take-over we were supposed to get the many things that we lacked (like three-quarters of the school buildings, which haven't even been started yet and probably never will be; or some textbooks; or some equipment or our laboratory; or in fact anything). In fact we seem to be getting less. It seems that Kaduna has just forgotten, or wants to forget, all about us. At the moment I am trying to shape the first eleven up for the first round of the Northern Nigeria schools soccer competition. The team is pretty good . . . [but] . . . we have no transport or money to take the boys anywhere and so have to wait for the Sokoto schools to come down and play us. At the moment however there is a little problem. We don't have a football in the school. As usual something went wrong with the order. Something always goes wrong with the order. . . .'

The beginning of the school year could be upsetting to a girl unprepared for the hazards of life in East Africa:

'As the poor kids drifted in, mattresses were unrolled and placed on sacking on the floor of the Assembly Hall – which had been divided by bamboo fencing into a classroom, with no desks, and a dormitory. We soon had a place which resembled the London Underground during the war: 25 poor little dears sleeping cheek by jowl on the floor. But they were lucky – we had also been forced to take a day stream who soon had our ears and hearts burning with stories of the fearful conditions in which they were living. Most of them sharing rooms with single men, many of whom get drunk and bring other women in. . . .'

119

By the end of the year most volunteers have learned to be philosophical, like the boy who wrote before leaving a school run by the Salvation Army in Malaysia:

'The school will remain open next year if the framework holds together. The hardboard partitions between the classrooms are now full of holes, having been eaten away by white ants, and part of the roof of the Captain's quarters collapsed yesterday, no doubt due to the same pest and aided by the rats that seek refuge up there from our watchdogs. I think G. (another volunteer) and I have the most stable quarters, though a fine mist descends on our beds whenever it rains, at which time we get out of bed and move to another part of the room.'

The physical challenge, clearly, is often considerable, involving not only a measure of personal discomfort but the difficulty of teaching without any of the material aids which could lessen the handicap of inexperience. Where these go hand in hand with human problems of apathy or hostility, the most hardened teacher from a secondary modern school in an industrial slum area might quail before some of the obstacles which volunteers have faced. In Bolivia, for instance, a 19-year-old girl found herself fighting this kind of battle on two fronts. Her main duty was to teach English to young trade unionists at a college in Cochabamba, where her evening classes were 'a joy and fillip at the end of the day'. But in the daytime she divided her time between teaching English to medical students at the university and lending a hand at the local government primary school. The medical students were hostile:

'Three weeks ago we went once more to the faculty to try to give an exam to these 150 odd males – simply an exam to grade them into groups – and we had a virtual riot on our hands. Shouts, catcalls, whistles and chants of "we don't want English" – until we were torn between fury and female tears. Most of the exam papers came in with "I don't know or want to know English", or rude words in Quichina . . . .'

While at the primary school she reported:

'These little scraps come to school dirty and often unbreakfasted. . . . The children's poverty is almost without exception displayed in their head irritations and diseases, in growths on their hands and of course ragged clothing. Nor is it simply holy poverty with angelic faces smiling through the grime; the only discipline they receive at home and at school is the stick, and their not so attractive naughtiness is gauged to continue right up to that pitch. . . . Teaching is whittled down to the most basic English and half the lesson is spent in imposing some semblance of order.'

At first sight that might seem too challenging a situation to present to a volunteer, and a 'cadet' at that. But youth has its advantages, if it goes hand in hand with character and real ability, and Alison had all three. Speaking fluent Spanish she quickly learned to penetrate the barriers of her environment, to understand and sympathise with the causes of the discontent and unhappiness about her. Active at all sorts of levels in a community in which she won acceptance and whose 'sincerity and warmth' she learned to value, she wrote at the end that:

'With all the ups and downs, the frustrations and shortcomings, this *has* been a tremendous experience, whose value for me I could never repay. In nearly every aspect of my work and social contact here, I feel that for the little I give I get back a hundredfold; a most humbling sensation.'

It is in the nature of things that the younger volunteers, the ones without degrees or diplomas or teacher's certificates, should find themselves in some of the toughest teaching assignments, since they go in general to the poorer parts of the developing world and to the least well-endowed schools. Yet it is remarkable how seldom these school-leavers, the direct descendants of Dickson's original volunteers, are troubled by problems of indiscipline – or at least fail to overcome them. A part of the explanation must lie in their very youth, in the fact that their readiness to join on equal terms in the life of their pupils gives them an advantage which would be denied to anyone older and correspondingly more inhibited. Often, but by no means always, they

121

are helped by the fact that their pupils genuinely and urgently want to learn, that mathematics or the intricacies of English grammar, as the touchstones of advancement, sometimes inspire in the new world a yearning which would be unusual in the old. Where this is not so, the success of a cadet volunteer is likely to depend on his ability to adapt himself to his surroundings and to see life through the eyes of his pupils – and at 18 or 19 that is something which he will never find as easy again. One volunteer wrote at some length of the difficulties of school-teaching in Algeria and then, feeling that he had been too hard on pupils who were un-disciplined but never uninterested, he added:

'But I hope I haven't painted them too darkly. Generally, they are extremely amusing to teach – far more so perhaps than an English class. And of course out of school when you don't have to quell this – call it vitality if you like – they are by and large delightful. In other words, I suppose they haven't been put through the wringer of English school discipline and are a bit less dehydrated as a result. And this has advantages and disadvantages.'

A girl who had been teaching in Sabah was more explicit in saying what was required of a volunteer in her situation. Writing to advise VSO about her successor, she said:

'Please send someone with a sense of humour, someone who won't mind having a go at anything from hair-cutting and burying pigs which are bad to helping in the dispensary – in fact almost anything – and who doesn't mind being isolated, and the numerous complications which come with isolation – and who will accept the river trip as an everyday way of travelling, who genuinely loves children and has the patience of a hundred and to make her a "Miss Ideal", someone who isn't sarcastic. . . .'

For a peculiarly exacting teaching project in Labrador, VSO found something very close to a 'Miss Ideal'. Sandra was unusual for a cadet in that she was 21 and had worked for a year or two as a secretary before applying to VSO. With two other volunteers, both boys who had just left school, she was posted to a mission school for Eskimo children, where the three of them found themselves almost at once in sole charge. The environment seemed as unpromising as it could well be and it was not difficult to see why the school failed to attract regular teachers:

'There is absolutely no incentive here for the children to work. It is almost impossible to communicate with the parents, who do not speak English. . . . To create a desire for learning is the great problem; the children do not want to learn, they lack ambition and an aim in life – the boys just want to log, fish and hunt like their fathers, and the girls to become housewives. Even if they wanted to learn, there would still be the problems resulting from their home life to cope with.'

Wretched poverty, unemployment, drunkenness – even incest – provided a sombre background to the life of the Eskimo children, most of whom were undernourished and many demoralised by the conditions in which they lived. The three volunteers did what they could for them within the framework of the life of the school, but quickly realised that if they were to have any lasting effect on the life of the community they must look beyond their immediate horizon:

'On the Friday after Christmas, following much hesitation and debate, we had a party in the school and invited 32 young people from the village. All came, to our astonishment, and a few more besides, and the evening was such an encouraging success that we were convinced that a youth club *would* work here. We began work in the old school room, which was lying waste, repaired the stove, wired the place for electricity, and generally changed what was once a dreary classroom into a cosy club-room, with scrubbed floors and walls decorated by photos and appropriate titles cut out of *Telegraph* and *Observer* supplements. . . .'

The youth club was a startling success, and it provided an illustration of a truth which applies to the work of all volunteers, but particularly (as the girl in Sabah suggested) to that of the cadets. Outside activities of every kind, whether within the life of a school or in the wider life of the community beyond it, form an essential part of the ideal volunteer project. An appetite for this kind of involvement, a willingness to turn his hand to anything, is indeed the distinguishing mark of the volunteer, who has entered into no limited contract to perform certain specific duties and no others, but who offers certain modest qualifications in return for the chance to gain experience of another world. Sometimes the bargain works out unexpectedly, as it did for Charles, another cadet volunteer, who was teaching at a school in the Cameroun and who had this experience when he embarked on a bus journey across the Nigerian border:

'I clambered over 44 legs to my seat and was just about to fall asleep, when I was awoken by screams and shouts. A pregnant woman had begun to have her labour pains. "Que faire?" Everyone was in a state of panic – including me, but my British sangfroid came to my rescue. I rang the bell telling the driver to stop, but he wouldn't. This being so I decided to deliver the baby myself! I made her drink as much palmwine as possible as an anaesthetic. Then I made everyone clear out of the way. The poor woman clung to my sore ribs so tightly, that I was undoubtedly in more agony than she was – only a supposition as I have never had to face the same experience. After 2 hours the baby started to come out feet first. Unabashed I helped it out and then patted it on the back (seen all that on the tele). The brat immediately started to howl, which only added to the confusion. However the problem now was to cut the cord. I procured a pen knife, which I cauterised with matches, then tying the cord in the middle, delicately slashed both ends. Then I put a banana leaf on the open flesh and tied it with a shoelace. The next job was to persuade the mother to eject all the accompanying extraneous matter. This she did very unwillingly as the Africans think it bad ju-ju if it comes out, and they go to great lengths to keep it in the mother's womb.

After my hard work, I took a well earned cigarette, and in between puffs was obliged to keep the woman from standing up. When I arrived at my destination I hastened to find a taxi, but the woman preferred to walk, but was finally coerced by brute force on my part – I also had to pay for it. Any chance of reimbursement? Last thing I heard was that mother and progeny were doing fine and they had decided to christen it Charles.'

After that it seems superfluous to insist that even with the expansion of the programme for qualified volunteers, from other countries as well as Britain, there is still a place for the school-leaver. If some countries, whose rising standards of education have carried them well along the road of development, are now looking only for qualified help, there are others who still have further to go. For them, the intelligent school-leaver has plenty to offer both in the way of academic achievement and still more in all-round usefulness as an agent of change, an initiator of new ideas and a link between the rising generations of the old world and the new. In this context youth and inexperience, and even the lack of higher qualifications, can all be assets, giving the volunteer a freedom of action which age and status must tend to limit. If, in addition to two or three 'A' levels, a boy has been a scout, or passed through the Duke of Edinburgh's Award Scheme, or has some practical aptitude or skill which he can pass on to his pupils – or if a girl, at the age of 18 or so, can add music or a knowledge of First Aid or domestic science to the ability to teach in the lower reaches of a secondary school – there are plenty of openings where this kind of 'unqualified' help may make all the difference for a remote community between having its children taught by amateurs and not having them taught at all.

Such is the situation in the Falkland Islands, where a couple of thousand farmers and fishermen inhabit a tiny archipelago three hundred miles from the mainland of South America. Their scattered homesteads and the broken nature of the countryside present special problems for the education of children already isolated from the mainstream of world events. For the professional teacher the attractions of so remote a post are few; there is neither the intellectual challenge nor the compensation of an absorbing environment to make recruitment easy. But for the volunteer whose own recent schooldays equip him to teach 'the basic primary subjects, arts and crafts and a little general science', the peculiar conditions of the teacher's life in the Falkland Islands are a posi-tive inducement. His pupils do not gather to meet him in a school-room. Instead he must go to find them in their homes, travelling from one homestead to another on horseback – sometimes by launch or Land Rover or even in a light aircraft – staying a few days in each and setting them homework (and coaching the parents in its supervision) to be picked up and corrected when next he reaches this point on his erratic circuit. 'Good mixers essential', says the project request form submitted annually to VSO by the Superintendent of Education in Port Stanley, capital of the island dependency – meaning that once the homework is disposed of and plans for the future mapped out, the volunteer can be pretty sure of being asked to shear a sheep or two, or to lend a hand with the fencing, before he takes a last look at the Southern Cross and turns in for the night.

Islands have an appeal for most of us, but whether it is Robert Louis Stevenson or Robinson Crusoe who is at the back of our minds few of them on closer acquaintance live up to their romantic promise. Hurricanes, poverty, tropical ulcers and tribal super-stitions too often – as many volunteers have learned – lie not far behind the palm trees fringing the blue lagoon. In the Solomon Islands, on New Guinea, in the Seychelles, even in the Caribbean, where the travel agents cast their sometimes deceptive spells, there are cadet volunteers working amongst some of the most under-privileged communities on earth. Here again the volunteer's opportunity lies in the fact that teaching demands a good deal more than the professional might care to offer: digging drains, nursing the sick, rebuilding the school after a storm, teaching everything from English and arithmetic to handicraft, art and nature study, supervising health and physical education classes, running debates – and all this in a climate of which one girl advised her successor (from Bougainville in the territory of Papua and New Guinea) 'it's as in the geography books, try to keep thinking of something else'. Mail had to be collected from the post office 'only 8 miles away'; and as it had been a very dry year, clothes had to be taken a couple of miles to be washed in the river; then in the next letter she was writing of floods and of a visit to a pupil in hospital: 'I walked there when the rains stopped, about 16 miles there and back, but up to my thighs for half of it. . . . I felt very fine on return however'.

These are examples of one kind of challenge, a challenge which can be exhilarating, but also daunting to the volunteer who is unprepared for it. Nor is it easy to describe it faithfully to someone who has as yet no experience of it and no yardstick by which to judge its effects in advance. (The only person qualified to do so is another volunteer who has experienced the same situation.) But in situations where the volunteer faces this kind of discomfort, whether mental or physical, it is seldom the discomfort itself which constitutes the essence of the challenge. Much more important is the question of whether, in such a situation, the volunteer can be of use or not. Difficult conditions, a sordid environment, actual hardship, will be rendered tolerable or intolerable by the value the volunteer is able to place on his or her own presence, by the usefulness of the job to be done, its relevance to the environment, and the qualifications of the volunteer to do it.

Precisely the same is true of situations where the challenge is a quite different and more subtle one, as it is today for an increasing number of volunteers, and especially for many of the qualified teachers. VSO in its maturity has inherited from its early self a curious handicap, in the shape of a public image which is romantic, even exotic, and which is heavily tinged with extremes of individualism and enterprise. It will be sad indeed, and strange, if these qualities ever cease to be associated with an enterprise to which, as we have seen, they are so essential; but it is also the fact that in many of the situations that confront volunteers today – and more especially the volunteers who go to teach – these are not necessarily the principal requirements. An excess of individualism may indeed impair the usefulness of a volunteer, who is called upon to serve, whether as a teacher or as anything else, within the framework of an established institution. There are circumstances where enterprise alone, without the judicious ballast of application and a willingness to accept orders, can even do more harm than good. In recruiting volunteers for these situations VSO today has to contend with its own legend, has to run the risk of disappointing those who would welcome the most rugged form of challenge, by offering them something which is not often

127

easier – indeed, it is almost always a more exacting form of service – but which strikes in the youthful imagination a note of less exhilarating alarm.

The risk was well expressed by a graduate working in Malaysia, a girl who was sent to teach English in a boys' school in Kelantan:

'When I read of volunteers who are doing real pioneer work in incredibly difficult conditions my imagination is stirred and I long to build a runway, start a welfare centre or organise a youth club; but I have come to accept that such trail-blazing will not be for me nor for someone who comes to continue this project. Firstly, these things and many more like them have been done by local people. But, more importantly, teaching in its widest sense is a full-time job. . . . I have come to the conclusion that the best and most valuable thing I can do is to teach English and to teach it to the very best of my ability – and that any regular, committed spare-time activities should be related to it in some way.'

This problem of adjustment is all the harder for volunteers who go to teach in countries relatively well-off but where, for one reason or another, it is still difficult to find a sufficient number of capable teachers. Singapore presents an example, where volunteers have often felt on arrival that VSO had misjudged its purpose and their own. The schools are well organised and generally well staffed. The Chinese community is, in Asian terms, affluent. The Europeans, service families and businessmen, look with some mistrust on the young volunteers whose approach to the local population is so different from their own. There is at first sight little justification for placing volunteers in this situation, which is psychologically a difficult one for them and would be overwhelmingly so if they were not persuaded of their own usefulness. Let one of them speak for herself:

'I expect everyone has written about the need, or lack of need, for VSO in Singapore. As I see it, there is a definite need, though in a different and more subtle way. This is not an under-developed country, where teachers literally cannot be found, although there is of course a shortage, particularly to teach the higher classes. We are needed in other ways. Firstly, I hope, we help to counteract

128

the idea that all Europeans are like some of the service families here, who act as if they were far better than the locals and behave far worse and never mix with Singaporeans. Secondly, in the schools we who are only here for a short time have the energy to teach enthusiastically in spite of the large classes, and to treat people as individuals, which I think is valuable. Many local teachers succumb to the unequal struggle of classes of 45 or over and inadequate equipment just to get through lessons and do no more than the bare minimum. Thirdly, as English teachers we are undoubtedly useful since (as is everywhere acknowledged) the standard of English is dropping and the English spoken by many is becoming more difficult to understand.'

She adds, on a note which is echoed by the volunteers from very many countries, that for herself she values the experience she gained in Singapore because 'nobody could have been kinder, friendlier or more welcoming than our fellow-teachers at the schools', and there is a reminder here of the sentiment expressed by George Edinger ten years earlier, when he wrote of the hostility we had aroused in Asia by adopting the attitudes of 'a superior and privileged people.' To modify that hostility, to do something positive to turn it into understanding and sympathy, is a worthwhile end in itself – and volunteers in Singapore have also found, in addition to their work as teachers, unusually varied opportunities to involve themselves in social work among blind or handicapped children and in the poorer strata of urban society.

Here again, as with the cadets, the key to a volunteer's success lies often in the range of his aptitudes and interests in addition to the classroom work he is qualified to undertake. In all but the most highly organised schools in most African and Asian countries there is likely to be endless scope for volunteers to join in, or perhaps to initiate, the kind of activities which are familiar in an English school: the debates and discussion groups, the drama societies, the scientific or photographic clubs, the orchestra or choir – and to lend to these the enthusiastic attention for lack of which they have so often lapsed into bored inaction or else never been undertaken at all. This kind of extra-curricular contribution, and the energy that goes with it, the volunteer is especially qualified to provide; and the need for such assistance can transform an otherwise indifferent project into one where a volunteer can be particularly valuable. A good girls' school in West Pakistan, for instance, adequately equipped and well run, with a measure of government support, might at first seem to offer little opportunity for a volunteer; but the graduate who went to teach there found otherwise, writing:

'The school has every facility and is very well staffed. There are two other teachers of English, both very competent. Basically I have a relatively easy timetable, until you add school magazines, debates, outings, plays and a choir. . . .'

At a grammar school in Northern Nigeria, a science teacher found himself helping also with the teaching of English, geography and music, until he had more classroom periods than any other member of the staff – but in addition:

'The school library became my domain and the revising of the old lending system. With that came the responsibility for producing this year's school magazine, the formation of the school "choir", helping to run the scout troop, organising school photographs and their distribution, the post of staff secretary, assistant games master, organiser of end-of-term activities and eventually Inspector of Schools during the School Cert. exams. All in all my feelings were thrown into the melting pot early and they have come out modified, wiser, frustrated, but happy.'

Of course, things do not always work out so comfortably, and the note of frustration is a recurrent one, reflecting the fact that precisely because the volunteers go out expecting to be used in a dozen ways by far-sighted principals, they are sometimes doomed to disappointment. From a secondary school in Libya a disillusioned volunteer in 1965 reported that:

'The school opened officially on October 4th, when a few dozen pupils turned up. This didn't perturb the headmaster, who calmly remarked that perhaps they would come the next day – or the next week. By the end of October we generally had full classes,

130

but this lost a month in teaching time, and out of the next seven months of the year we have lost innumerable days for frequent holidays declared out of the blue – often we turn up ourselves for classes and find no one around because a holiday has been declared suddenly for something. And now Ramadan has begun we are losing even more time because the students are just too tired to turn up.'

VSO no longer sends volunteers to Libya,[1] since the growth of its oil revenues should enable it to recruit all the teachers it needs—but the volunteer was only describing an extreme example of a situation that can develop anywhere. The answer to it, from VSO's point of view, lies first in the careful project selection for which it relies so much on the British Council. If a mistake has been made, or if a sudden decline sets in in what had appeared a suitable project (and this can happen for a variety of reasons in countries where the education system is subject to pressures unfamiliar to an English headmaster, from tribal jealousies to a drop in the world price of cocoa) VSO has always the option, though a reluctant one, of transferring a volunteer to a post where he will be better used. But the best solution lies with the volunteer himself, who will have been warned of the frustrations that may lie ahead and which are often an integral part of the challenge to his imagination as well as his ability. It is a solution whose exact form he will have to work out for himself and which may consist either in scaling down his ambitions or extending them, and whose success will depend ultimately on his character and on that central quality of adaptability, on which VSO inevitably lays such stress. The frustrations can be of all kinds—idle pupils, vacillating principals, inadequate facilities for proper teaching, cynicism or prejudice in the local environment – the list is endless, but there are few of them that cannot be mitigated, if not altogether overcome by the volunteer's willingness to adjust his ideas and his personality to the world about him.

It sounds, for instance, as though this girl teaching at a remote school in Nigeria sized up pretty quickly the effort required of her:

[1] Except to one technical school in Tripoli.

'I think it is very good for people to be able to teach here. It cures you of anger and of taking personal offence. The students find it funny if you get cross, so you don't – so in the end you don't need to. And a much happier relationship ensues. When you get somewhere, you really *do*.'

Faced with a more difficult situation in Pakistan, another girl was depressed to find so little echo there of the high ideals she had brought with her from England – and sensibly modified her original vision of swiftly changing the world:

'If at the end of the year I come away having made three or four good friends, and having left the girls whom I teach with a slightly clearer impression of what the West means (and a less strong loathing of the English language) then I shall feel the year has not been a waste. I am continually happy here because always busy. I *love* the teaching, so much so that I intend to continue with it on my return and have cancelled the place I had at Liverpool to do child care.'

The teaching posts open to volunteers vary enormously but these random examples indicate some of the characteristics common to a great many of them. If one tried to produce a kind of 'Identikit' blueprint of a representative teaching project, it would be something along these lines. A secondary school, probably state administered but quite possibly a mission foundation; more likely to be up-country in the 'bush' or its local equivalent (because the up-country school finds it harder to attract the normal contract teacher, even if it can afford to pay one); with indifferent buildings and playing-fields, and probably little in the way of laboratory equipment or other specialised facilities. Its staff will include few members, whether indigenous or European, who have worked at the school for more than a year or are likely to be there in twelve months' time; a volunteer staying for two years may well find himself the senior member of the staff after the headmaster.[1] If there is a library, it probably needs restocking and a

[1] In 1968 one volunteer in his second year was acting as headmaster of a mission school in Rwanda.

complete overhaul of its filing and lending system – and if it does not, it is not unknown for it to be kept under lock and key 'to avoid damage to the books'. Games will most likely be run on haphazard lines with inadequate equipment, and there will probably be little else in the way of 'outside activities' to relieve the tedium of a system of education conceived and understood, by teachers and pupils alike, as a contrivance for the negotiation of examination hurdles.

Within this pattern there are endless variations – and outside it as well. The problems of education are not the same in every part of the developing world, and the differences are reflected in the distribution of volunteers and in the nature of the work they do. In Africa, which absorbs the greater part of VSO's teaching volunteers, there is in general a straightforward shortage of qualified teachers of every kind, while in many African countries the language of instruction is English and curricula are modelled on the English pattern. There are in consequence relatively few problems about fitting English-speaking volunteers into an education system which is under constant strain but which every African government is eager to expand.

India and Pakistan, where education is concerned, are in an altogether different situation from the emergent countries of Africa. Not so much in the proportion of their populations which receive any education at all, which – in very rough terms – is much the same in India and in Africa; but in the fact that both India and Pakistan have a relatively high proportion of university graduates, where most African countries have woefully few. Does it make any sense, therefore, for volunteers from Britain, whether qualified or not, to serve in Indian schools, especially when their ignorance of the local languages restricts them for the most part to the 'better' schools (some of them state-run, some private) where the medium of instruction is English? Would it be better to concentrate them all in Africa or in the other countries which lack India's strongly developed (some would say over-developed) pattern of higher education?

There is no easy answer to these questions, which preoccupy

VSO. (This was what I meant by saying earlier that there was a certain 'waywardness' about the geographical distribution of its volunteers.) There are already about ten times as many volunteers in Africa as in India, although India's population is half as large again as that of the combined African states. If the volunteers were removed from India, they would leave only the most insignificant of gaps on its broad grey surface. Yet there are arguments which are not merely sentimental for retaining this minor aspect of a connection both long-standing and affectionate. The Indian headmasters who employ them look to the volunteers for something which an Indian teacher could not provide: something, it may be, which is out of date and which (and this is perhaps more important) the volunteers may be shy of offering. One might call it simply 'Englishness': an English approach, an English way of tackling problems, not least an English way of speaking English.

Now this may be touching; it can also be embarrassing. It masks in some cases a simple snobbery and it has little to do with the underlying purpose of VSO, though it does not necessarily conflict with it. It raises questions, which only Indians can answer, about the kind of society that modern India is aiming to create. And it should not blind us to the fact that volunteers working in Indian schools and travelling vast distances during their holidays (usually in the great inexpensive democracy of third class on the Indian railways) have an opportunity to rub shoulders with the real India from which few of them fail to profit. Nor, surely, does India herself? Describing his own travels in India, one unusually perceptive volunteer wrote:

'Lack of money meant that I had to live cheaply and therefore I was not cut off from the country's reality. . . . Everywhere I met with the greatest friendship, though some surprise that I should be travelling 3rd class. Many invited me to share meals or stay at their villages. But normally I ate for a few shillings on railway stations or in bazaars and I slept where I could: in pilgrim's rest-houses at temples, stations waiting rooms or railway roofs, cheap hotels or government rest houses, on a house-boat on the Dal lake, in a tent in the Himalayas, at a tiny bazaar stall in Kerala, or

134

for a rupee on a hotel corridor floor at Cape Comorin and, of course, on trains – albeit in luggage racks or under the seats.'

In the heyday of the travel agents and their package tours, this has an invigorating ring – and there is nothing transitory about the effects of such an experience, which are indeed incalculable:

'India is now a part of my life, a force that has shaped me, as much a part of my experience as my home town in Wales. Newspaper reports on India now have urgency and relevance. I own Indian literature, from the Bhagawat-Gita to Nirad Chaudhuri. Intellectually the year was worth two at university, but there is more to it than this. Having lived in an alien community and culture, I see our own in clearer perspective. I can more easily distinguish the essential from the transient. But perhaps the essence of the year is summed up in a remark made to me by a teacher brought up under the Raj: "Excuse me, please, for saying so, but you are not like other Englishmen, and that is really very wonderful, isn't it?" '

Implicit here is the dual nature of the volunteer's task. It is expected of him that he be capable of filling a useful role as a teacher; it is also expected that he should seize the opportunity to establish a new kind of relationship with those among whom he is living and working. To enable him to do both effectively demands constant enterprise and experiment on the part of VSO in the choice of projects, and in trying to diversify its work in India, VSO has discovered openings as far removed as they could well be from the 'better schools' with their Westernised approach. One such is Gandhigram, a rural institute in South India, which is part of a wider community to which the central government has recently accorded the status of a Rural University. The purpose of the institute is the regeneration of the Indian social order along the lines laid down by Mahatma Gandhi, and the Gandhian principles of non-violence and social justice are fundamental to its character. So is the aim of self-sufficiency, the idea that a rural community, even while it tries to educate its members to share in a fuller life, should continue to meet its own needs through

135

agriculture and rural industries. Including as it does a hospital, a birth-control centre and various social and material welfare services, Gandhigram is in fact a broadly based experiment in social education, which functions against the wholly practical background of an Indian rural community. Here is one of the more exacting of VSO's projects for graduate volunteers, calling for conformity to inflexible principles in matters of diet and social intercourse, and a willingness on the part of the young Englishman to integrate himself with a community alien in character and outlook to anything in his experience. The setting of Gandhigram is splendid, its atmosphere austere, and it offers to the volunteer not only a straightforward teaching job but also a chance to look below the surface of Indian life, and in some measure to become for a time a part of it.

Qualified volunteers have been working at Gandhigram since 1964, and more recently another promising project has been initiated at the Punjab Institute of English at Chandigarh. Here, unusually, VSO has sent not a single volunteer but a team of eight, who attended a special training course in India and are working with a larger group of Canadian volunteers, with the object of raising the standard of English teaching in secondary schools throughout the Punjab. These are all qualified teachers who have undertaken to serve for two years, and there are clear arguments for using such volunteers (in India and elsewhere) within the framework of education programmes worked out by higher institutes of this kind. There is also plenty of scope in teacher training colleges overseas, where volunteers with the necessary degree of professional competence can make a wider contribution than would be possible in a single school; and the expansion of this side of VSO's work has gone hand in hand with a steady increase in the number of volunteers recruited from Colleges of Education in Britain, whose training makes them particularly useful in posts of this kind. In the rapid expansion of education programmes in the developing countries, teacher training colleges obviously have a key role to play. In raising their standards, VSO – which now draws more than a third of its qualified teaching volunteers from the Colleges of Education – is well placed to help, especially with the teaching of English.

Every year VSO recruits a number of teachers with a few years of experience behind them and these are valuable in filling the more specialised posts open to volunteers. There are, for instance, university posts in the Philippines, in Ghana and in Thailand, and there are opportunities in the current development of educational broadcasting in many countries. Here again, training and ability can be used on the widest scale, and there are volunteers engaged in this kind of work in East and West Africa, in Singapore and Fiji, in the Sudan and in Guyana. There are openings, too, in the teaching of the blind, often sadly neglected in the developing countries. At the moment a young woman, with five years of teaching experience and a certificate from the Guildhall School of Music and Drama, is serving in a new project in a remote part of Kenya, a blind school where she teaches English and music, helps with the drama society and the school choir and is the only English person on the staff. Within a month of her arrival in the autumn of 1967 she had decided to stay for two years, and presently she was exploring the possibility of working for a further two years on contract after that. At a similar project in Tanzania another girl, who is herself blind, has been working in the country's first school for blind pupils, teaching in Swahili and touring the nearby villages as a living demonstration to African parents that the handicap of blindness need not prevent their children from receiving and making use of an education. In these and other teaching projects at every level, volunteers have found opportunities to join in evening classes or in other activities, formal or informal, which serve the common purpose of furthering education as an aspect of social development. From Ghana a graduate with a full timetable of classroom work at a teacher training college writes:

'The latest addition has been two periods of oral English at a nearby Presbyterian seminary. When I arrived for the first lesson, I thought I had gone to the wrong place. There was a roomful of old men all dutifully standing up and chorusing "Good After-

137

noon, Sir". Investigation showed that the youngest was 55 and the oldest 62. Since most of them have been speaking English about twice as long as I have, it isn't very easy to change their habits.'

Amidst all this variety there are bound to be some false starts and a good deal of frustration – sometimes more and sometimes less serious than the experience of the volunteer who spent a couple of months collecting material for a school magazine, only to see the precious manuscript eaten by goats on the eve of publication. Sometimes disillusionment will swamp the bright hopes with which a volunteer has set out, and where this happens, the blame may lie with VSO for placing the wrong volunteer in the wrong project, or even for taking on a project which was unsuitable in the first place. It may lie with the project, if it looks to the volunteer for something more or less than it is in his power to give. Or the volunteer himself may be at fault, through a lack of imagination or flexibility; but without these the selection board should never have chosen him to begin with. As one volunteer wrote from that project at Gandhigram, after his first bewildering experience of the complexities of Indian society, 'one can only try to understand'. And that is the essence of it, on which all the rest depends; that and a willingness to accept the frustrations and to be on the look-out for the opportunities when they present themselves. It would be foolish to pretend that because a volunteer is able and well-intentioned success will be automatic. But if the underlying willingness is there, and that central quality of adaptability, a volunteer will seldom find himself in a situation that cannot be turned to good account in one way or another.

The satisfactions that are open to him are various, and they will not always be those that he anticipated. A teacher can seldom expect dramatic results in a short time and if he goes out expecting to change the world, the volunteer is inviting disappointment. In the early days of VSO the Director of Education in one Asian territory expressed this in realistic terms, remarking of the volunteers who had worked in a school under his charge: 'they cannot build monuments that they can see to assess the value of their

138

work, but I, who have lived here longer, have been astonished by the effect that two years of volunteers in that school have been able to accomplish.'

What then are these accomplishments and these satisfactions likely to be? One could express them – though few volunteers would – in terms of a general whittling away of the obstacles rooted in ignorance, and of the help that volunteers can give to the developing countries on their slow, their sometimes imperceptible, advance towards a fuller life, whether that life be conceived in terms of higher material standards of living or of wider horizons for the mind. One could talk of the friendships made and the connections established, in the light of which the deceptions of prejudice and convention are witheringly exposed. One could point to the opportunities for self-knowledge and fulfilment, the chance for the individual to assess his own capabilities, to learn what it is he looks for in life and what the world can expect of him. All this, I believe, would be justified – but if one asks the volunteers themselves, the answers are likely to be less pretentious, more specific and personal and modest. From Nigeria, for instance:

'I am certainly glad that I was posted into "the bush" rather than given a place in one of the towns. . . . Now that I can look at life here more as a part of it than as an intruder, I wonder at the dignity and cheerfulness that I find in these people, who have really so little to be cheerful about. After the quiet, intimate and seemingly chaotic life of the bush, the garishness of the town tires and irritates me and I'm always glad to get *home*.'

The italics are mine – but the note is a familiar one, and it is echoed by this girl teaching at a secondary school in Ghana:

'Our Christmas dinner was chicken stew and *fufu* eaten from a communal pot, sitting round a stool discussing the variations in the colour of our skins! Somehow I was glad not to be joining in the overeating and waste that goes on at home. If I had my way, this is how I would always spend such an occasion, sitting in a mud hut, amongst people who have so much to give and yet have so little. I have never felt so happy on Christmas Day before.'

139

The warmth that comes of acceptance into an alien community, and the establishment of a relationship that owes nothing to convention, is one important element; and the other is the sense of a job worth doing, as another girl found in Malaysia:

'I had not imagined that I could become involved in teaching so that it really mattered to me if I did not put everything into my lessons or if I felt that my students were not getting the very best I can give them. In view of this I am hoping to stay on here until December so that I can complete the academic year and feel that for the first time I have completed some small job of work.'

And from the Sudan:

'At the moment I am the only physics and chemistry master in a school of 300 boys thirsting for knowledge. I am quite excited by the prospect of reorganising the laboratories, and especially by one piece of equipment . . . a gas generator costing well over £200. Ever since it arrived, it has been lying in the store, neglected because nobody could assemble it. I hope to do so, and to allow the boys to do their own experiments with bunsen burners, rather than just watching the teacher.'

There may be nothing as concrete as this, nothing more precise than the consciousness of a need met or the sense of being extended for a purpose that is basically worth while. And if he is lucky the volunteer may get an occasional bonus, of the kind that came the way of this graduate at a Teacher Training College in Ghana:

'I wanted to introduce the 4th year to some poetry and to kindle some feeling for the sound of words. After a lot of thought I had Henry V's speech before Harfleur cyclostyled. When I circulated it there were gasps – was this English? Then I read it through, really hamming it. This had a great reception. In all, I read it through four times straight off before the cries of "Again, Again" subsided. The next day the students were out clearing the bush on the new site. What should I hear but "Once more into the breach" coming from half a dozen places in the bush? Waving their machetes as they shouted "God for Harry . . ." they really looked the part! I felt very pleased when I realised that I had "got through" to them.'

And if these scattered comments take too little account of the complaints and the frustrations which also find plenty of expression, let's leave the last word to another volunteer in West Africa, who told a long tale of woe and concluded:

'Although things might sound grim from this letter, I can assure you that I wouldn't swap places with anyone in England just at the moment.'

Chapter 9

Volunteers in Development Work

'Travel in the younger sort, is a part of education.' Few of us would challenge Bacon's judgment – and while he might have modified it, had he lived to see coachloads of English tourists debouching on the Costa Brava only to demand fish and chips and bingo, the principle still holds good.

What Bacon meant, of course, was that it is impossible for us, particularly when we are young, to move about the world without picking up something that will add to our sum of knowledge, our awareness of the world in which we live, but of which we are only *at home* in one small corner. Perhaps it is worth while to carry the argument a stage further, to suggest that if travel confers this considerable benefit on those who are able to undertake it, we should try to make it, quite literally, a part of education, by introducing it into the curriculum of our schools or universities. The idea is attractive, and if it raises certain practical problems, why, VSO and the other organisations operating along similar lines offer a blueprint for their solution. More than once it has been suggested that the introduction of some form of 'civil conscription', of national service directed to the aims of peace rather than of war, would revitalise our youth and give it a role to fill in the world.

This is not the place to examine the idea or to balance the loss of the voluntary impulse against the gain in sheer manpower which could be applied to solving the development problems of the world.

The point for the moment is that voluntary service, whether at home or abroad, is not charity, although charity enters into it. It is a form of bargain, involving benefits as well as obligations; and it is most often the case that the volunteer, no matter how faithfully he fulfils his side of the bargain, feels in the end that it is he who has benefited from it most.

This is most true – and it is not difficult to see why – of those whom VSO calls its development volunteers. It may apply equally well to many of the teachers; but then, of the volunteers who go overseas to teach, by no means all intend to make teaching their eventual career. For the rest, there is experience to be gained, certainly, in the wider sense; it can hardly be wasted and it may prove to be of great value and unexpected relevance, perhaps even deciding them in the choice of a career. But for the great majority of the development volunteers (those, broadly speaking, who go to work on other than classroom teaching projects), their period of service overseas will be directly related to their later careers. They will indeed have been selected because they possess certain qualifications or aptitudes, by the exercise of which they intend eventually to earn their daily bread. The opportunity to exercise these skills and to sharpen them by instructing others in their use – all this in situations, as a rule, of particular urgency and challenge – constitutes indeed 'a part of education', as well as an invigorating apprenticeship in the arts of mature citizenship.

Numbering in all about 500, the development volunteers constitute a little over one-third of VSO's total strength, and they fall into four main categories. There are the medical volunteers, ranging from qualified doctors and dentists through every kind of medical auxiliary; those with experience or a specific training in some form of agriculture; industrial volunteers, including ex-apprentices, skilled craftsmen and qualified engineers; and a mixed bag of people with qualifications in other fields closely related to the general purposes of development – social workers, librarians, specialists of one kind and another who are particularly hard to find in the developing countries. The conditions under

143

which these development volunteers live and work vary very widely, embracing the 'mud-hut' pattern which is many people's erroneous concept of the typical volunteer situation but including also many environments which surprise the volunteers by their level of sophistication.

The largest of these categories is that of the agriculturalists – and this is appropriate, since the developing countries are themselves agricultural societies, whose best prospect of supporting their own growing populations lies in the modernisation of their techniques of food production. The volunteers in this field may be university graduates, serving in research establishments or higher technical institutes. They may hold degrees or diplomas from Agricultural Colleges, or certificates from Farm Institutes in Britain. They may be foresters or biologists or fish farmers, and in a few cases they may have no more to offer – on paper – than 'A' level science, but reinforced by the practical experience of life on a farm, or the precious knowledge of how to use and maintain modern farm equipment.

Where there is such variety, both in the work to be done and in the qualifications for doing it, it is not easy to choose a thoroughly representative volunteer project; yet since a large proportion of agricultural volunteers are attached to government departments in East and Central Africa, it is appropriate to start with a project sponsored by Oxfam in Tanzania, where a 21-year-old girl from the Lancashire Institute of Agriculture was posted as assistant to a regional agricultural officer in Moshi. She held a diploma in dairying, and her first five weeks in Tanzania were spent learning Swahili at a course organised by the British Council for some sixty volunteers posted to different parts of East Africa. Then, after a few valuable days with the girl whom she was replacing, Vera settled into quarters provided by the local girls' school and took stock of her situation. Her first impressions were of the beauty of her surroundings on the slopes of Mount Kilimanjaro, and of the friendly welcome she received from the cattle-owning tribesmen of the area. A month or two later she was writing to VSO:

144

'I am finding my work more and more interesting as I get to know the farmers. My main work up here is to supervise a pilot Artificial Insemination scheme, help to arrange meetings for the local cattle society and give advice in the management of exotic dairy cattle in the area.'

Her immediate task was to get to know the ninety local farmers who belonged to the cattle society, making records, introducing new techniques and giving advice where it was needed – and here came the first lesson:

'We are achieving results in quite a few cases, especially those which we can follow up within a week or so after the first visit. I have discovered that if field officers are able to make follow-up visits the farmers will carry out advice – but if they think we are not coming again they don't bother to help themselves.'

At the girls' school she found 'a great shortage of teachers' and presently she was coopted as a games mistress and invited to help in running a Girl Guide company. After that there was silence for several months, during which Vera decided she was too much involved in what was going on around her to come home at the end of the twelve months and asked to extend her stay for a second year. By now she was on easy terms with all the local farmers and sufficiently at home in Swahili to be able to put her knowledge of dairy farming to really effective use. The standard of animal husbandry in the Kilimanjaro district showed a marked improvement, the artificial insemination scheme was well launched and Vera was busy instructing a number of junior agricultural officers to carry on the work after her return to England. The only cloud on the horizon was the thought of leaving 'my farmers – they are all so friendly now and treat me like one of the family', and when the two years were over and Vera left Tanzania a report on her work by the Principal Secretary of the Ministry of Agriculture remarked that 'her friendliness and good nature made her very welcome in farmers' homes and this contributed to her success as an extension worker'.

Over on the other side of Africa a very different type of work confronted Julian R., who had taken first class honours in Natural Science at Trinity College, Dublin, and who joined the Zoology department of the University of Ghana and worked on the Volta Dam Research Project. His time was divided between lecturing and research work at the university and trips up the lake to study fish resources and stocking problems. The scientific ramifications of the job fascinated him and he too found a year too short a stay. Well into his second year he was writing:

'December was spent doing the routine work that should have been done in November, and after a break of three days I was back on the lake again. Early next month I've got to give 8 lectures on Crustacea and take some practicals, so this is keeping me pretty busy at present. . . . Meanwhile the routine monthly research trips up the lake, lasting 8 to 10 days each, go on; I've been on all of them since last July and am looking forward to a break next month. As you may gather, I'm a bit overworked at the moment, as I collected more samples than I have time to analyse and get rather a lot of other jobs as well. I enjoy it very much indeed however, and am very glad to have come here.'

Six months later, with the end in sight, he surfaced from the long job of tabulating the results of his work on the research project:

'I've been working at top pressure, with the result that I finally got through the analysis of the last of 8000 fish today! I stink of, breathe, dream, think and talk fish, and am seriously thinking of vegetarianism and the contemplative life in some desert. But it's been very interesting and I've enjoyed it extremely.'

That was in the summer of 1967 and while it was the end of Julian's career as a volunteer his connection with Ghana was not broken. He was offered a research fellowship at the university and returned at the beginning of 1968 to resume his work on the lake and in the laboratory – not the only volunteer for whom VSO provided the starting-point in a career of service overseas.

A branch of agriculture of particular interest to many of the developing countries is forestry, and here again a period of service as a volunteer, far from being an irrelevance or a distraction for a young man who has chosen this for a career, can provide him with valuable experience while he helps in the vital work of preserving and developing what may be a young country's chief natural resource. University graduates and holders of certificates from the various Forestry Training Schools in Britain are working as volunteers in Malaysia, in the West Indies, and in half a dozen African countries, on all sorts of projects: lecturing, doing research, or helping with pilot schemes of afforestation or soil conservation. In Western Malaysia, for instance, where a succession of volunteers have served over the last few years at a Forestry Research Station, their work on pine trees as the basis for a pulping industry has prepared the ground for a pilot scheme which the World Bank has agreed to sponsor for three years from 1968.

Not all the development volunteers are working with government departments overseas. The specialists and the university graduates tend to be, because they possess qualifications which are urgently needed if national development plans are to bear fruit. But there are also private and philanthropic organisations all over the world trying on a smaller scale to tackle local problems of food production, and the related problems – which are basically those of education – which have to be solved if backward communities are to be taught to make the most of their environment and brought into the main stream of human progress.

Typical of these are the Cheshire Homes established in various countries to provide examples of small-scale development projects, where a fortunate few can gain some knowledge of basic techniques which they can then practise within their own local communities. There is one of these at Garfarsa, twenty miles outside Addis Ababa in the Ethiopian highlands, and it offers what is in many ways the ideal opening for a volunteer who has the essential technical equipment and the willingness of youth to become involved in every aspect of a situation where personality counts for much. Peter W., who had learned his agriculture in the East Riding of Yorkshire, found working here 'absolutely

147

the best thing I have done in my life – I LOVE it here!' Not that the life was easy or progress automatic:

'Problems are fantastic, numerous and very often apparently insoluble, but this is what makes life full of interest and keeps me busy. Although we are restricted somewhat by the lowering of our money reserves, the Garfarsa Home is now growing by leaps and bounds.'

This was a job for a jack-of-all-trades, and Peter, who had a Certificate of Agriculture, needed a good deal more besides, as this account of his work makes clear:

'As far as the running of the place goes: we have nearly finished the reservoir and the wiring of the house, this year's hay crop has been cut, the generator house has been built and the generator installed (though not wired up), loads of small jobs like cementing, painting, whitewashing, building, etc., have been completed, and our bee-house and bees are now functional. It will be a month or two before we get the cows in, as I'm not sure who I can trust to become cowman. I haven't time to milk and look after the cows completely.'

On a very different scale there are development projects in different parts of the world which aim to attack the underlying problems which restrict food production and the proper utilisation of natural resources. Dependent as they are on the use of modern techniques of mechanisation, and so on finding the skilled personnel capable of practising them, such schemes call for a combination of qualities and qualifications which the volunteer is often able to provide. Given the technical skill, the essential requirement for this kind of work, especially in its initial stages, may be the willingness to live hard and to face unexpected emergencies. In 1966, for instance, a number of agencies concerned with development work in India combined to sponsor a programme known as AFPRO (Action for Food Production). VSO provided two volunteers with an industrial background to help with a well-boring and irrigation project in Central India, which was being operated by the Church of Scotland Mission at Jalna, with financial help from Oxfam. Before going out to India they were carefully trained, first in the use of drilling rigs by the company in Halifax which had supplied the equipment for the project, and then by the army in the use of explosives. This enabled them, as soon as they arrived, to take over the maintenance of the mission's vehicles and equipment and to handle the well-boring and blasting operations. Then, when AFPRO launched an emergency well-drilling programme as part of the fight against the disastrous drought in Bihar, the volunteers flew to Bombay with an AFPRO team to collect three boring machines and three Land Rovers and helped to drive them a thousand miles north-east to Bihar, where AFPRO played a significant part in containing the disaster. The following year, more volunteers were requested and eventually the number engaged on the project rose to ten, all with an industrial background and five of them sponsored by sections of British industry.

The AFPRO project was an agricultural one, but these volunteers were among the fifty-odd directly sponsored by industrial firms in Britain. This pattern of industrial sponsorship has provided for VSO a most valuable source of manpower, both for practical projects of construction work, civil engineering or motor maintenance, and to meet the growing demand for instructors to teach in trade and technical schools all through the developing countries. The industrial ex-apprentice, with City & Guilds or equivalent qualifications, is ideally equipped to help in raising the level of technical proficiency in communities which urgently need this passport to the modern world. With his skill at his fingertips, trained to be resourceful and to find a practical application for his knowledge, the volunteer from industry is worth his weight in gold to societies lacking precisely these qualities in their approach to the business of development. And for the volunteers themselves – and their employers in Britain – this form of service offers a rare opportunity to develop self-assurance and initiative, and so to bring out the latent abilities of a young man who may not previously have had the chance to extend himself.

149

From the early days of VSO there had been ex-apprentices and other technical volunteers among each annual contingent: the first four went overseas in 1959, and it quickly became apparent that there was room for as many as British industry could be persuaded to spare. By 1965 the number had grown to 70 and with the demand increasing as rapidly, VSO took on its staff an industrial liaison officer with the special task of finding recruits from industry. With enthusiastic support from firms which had already released employees for a year's service, and by developing fresh contacts with a great many more, he was able to expand this side of VSO's operations until today there are nearly 150 of these technical volunteers in the field. One-third of these are ex-apprentices directly sponsored by their employers: the rest include technicians and craftsmen from almost every branch of industry, as well as university graduates in science or engineering. And even with this expansion VSO is able to meet only half of the requests which come in each year for help of this kind.

The most exhilarating aspect of life for many technical volunteers is that they learn to accept a degree of responsibility for which they might have to wait years at home. From Malaysia, for instance, one industrial volunteer writes that:

'The Tingi Hills are embraced by the Forest Reserve of Sanhan Biruva and completely inaccessible except on foot. There are also a lot of villages in the area completely isolated, so with Forestry Department money and chieftain labour I have been given the task of constructing two bridges which will open up the area. The job is quite a major construction programme – two concrete bridges spanning two rivers 18 and 23 feet wide and a lot of earth works. This must be finished before the rains in April or else we will all be washed out. The job is only just starting up but what with designing the bridges, getting out material quantities and supervising one hundred men I'm kept very busy. I never thought that my two years as a site engineer with Geo. Wimpey's would come in so useful – I don't think I'd have managed it otherwise as the bridges have to be of reinforced concrete.'

For an employer there are obvious advantages about a scheme

150

which can put such an opportunity in the way of a young man who has recently completed an industrial apprenticeship. Many of Britain's most progressive firms run training schemes for their employees, whose object is precisely to develop the qualities of initiative and self-reliance which are called for in the volunteer. One training officer has commented:

'It is a very worth while scheme indeed, and the benefits to the individual are considerable if he or she enters wholeheartedly into the spirit of the thing. There is a terrific opportunity to display initiative in civil engineering constructional schemes and educational experiments, in schools and technical colleges, in places well off the beaten track, without the frustrations and inhibitions of our own highly organised society.'

From the employer's point of view there is also a risk involved, in that the individual who enjoys this kind of opportunity may find it hard to settle down again to the routine of life in a large industrial concern. A measure of independence, in surroundings both challenging and invigorating, is not likely to leave a young man content to sink back into an environment which offers no comparable stimulus. Here the challenge is to industry itself and to our whole attitude towards the question of making proper use of our own human resources. What can hardly be questioned is the proposition that not only British industry but Britain itself has need of the qualities and the enterprise which this kind of service can foster. VSO, in its secondary aspect, presents a very practical form of training programme for the young recruit to industry; nor is this to lose sight of its primary purpose of providing the kind of specialised help which is needed by the developing countries as they grapple with the technical problems which stand in the way of their advance. In the ideal volunteer project, both aspects are combined, as they were for a young geologist from the Nottingham Regional College of Technology, who went to work on the development of water resources in Kenya:

'I go out on safari every week, either short trips (within a 50 mile radius of Nairobi) or longer ones which involve camping and spending 7 to 10 days in the bush. . . . My job becomes more interesting and absorbing every day – just my line and I intend to specialise in it when I return to the U.K. and university. Hydrology is a very important branch in the search for water, which is such an essential commodity in an arid country such as Kenya. So far I have had two boreholes drilled on sites which I had selected, both of which were extremely successful. I really feel that I'm doing a worth while job in a country which deserves all the help it can get.

'All the six months I've been here I've been my own boss, so I hold a fair amount of responsibility and authority which is very stimulating and makes life rather exciting. I could never hope to have a similar job at my age in the U.K., holding such an amount of responsibility.'

To those with more sedentary jobs, like the many volunteers teaching in trade schools and technical institutes anywhere from Jamaica to Thailand, there is an enviable quality about such projects as these, where the volunteer, whether he is clearing an airstrip in New Guinea or pushing a road through the mountains in Basutoland, can see the physical results of his efforts. Teaching, if it is not long since you were on the receiving end of it yourself, can be an intimidating business and many of the technical volunteers have accepted with initial misgivings their new status as instructors. As a rule, the misgivings fade soon enough – and what wins the day is usually a combination of two factors, both in evidence in the great majority of the situations in which these volunteers find themselves. There is, first, the eager welcome which greets them and the skills they have to communicate; and second, there is the realisation of the tremendous need for the help they have to offer. Working among people of their own age, they find that they win a ready acceptance – and are often startled to realise how limited are the horizons of their contemporaries in other countries:

'The majority of the students here' (writes a technical volunteer instructing in a trade school in Botswana) 'have never handled tools in their lives and have not had the opportunity of being brought up with and surrounded by furniture and other wooden fittings, as we in England have and which we take for granted. They are just not used to things being square, or to straight lines and the idea of accuracy.'

More than a suggestion there of the kind of difficulties that face some of these young instructors. Even where there is a real eagerness to learn, the results are often slow in coming and the pioneer in a project may feel discouraged by the lack of obvious progress. It may only be the volunteer who follows him who is able to detect the headway that is being made. A civil engineer teaching young Africans found himself building on the ground-work laid by others:

'All but four of my group have passed and are now able to sit their finals in December, which all points to the tremendous achievement of my predecessor. . . . I am finding the work much more satisfying than I ever imagined I would and it has shattered all my fears and premonitions. There is a tremendous challenge in putting over information, but when it lands fair and square and is accepted, then the whole effort is worth while and rewarding.'

For the technical volunteers the scope in the developing countries is apparently limitless; the problem is only to find them in sufficient numbers. Through all the pattern of economic development runs the constant theme of mechanisation, which offers a way of escape for peoples trapped by the physical or psychological limitations of their environment. With this process of emancipation volunteers are involved in all sorts of ways, helping to build schools, roads, bridges, hospitals; maintaining the vehicles of medical teams in Laos or of the Save the Children Fund in Jordan; producing maps for the malaria eradication programme in the Solomon Islands; installing the electrical equipment for a housing development in Peru – and everywhere teaching, at the work bench, in the laboratory, on the construction site, in many different countries and at various levels of technical advancement.

There is no area of life in the developing countries where

qualified help is more in demand than in the provision of proper medical services. Here, too, technical volunteers have proved themselves useful, like the ex-apprentices working in homes for the disabled in Ethiopia or with the Flying Doctor service in Kenya. And apart from auxiliaries like these VSO has steadily widened its recruitment of medical volunteers, who now comprise one quarter of those engaged on 'development' (as opposed to academic) projects and include men and women with every kind of qualification, from the fully fledged doctor or dentist to the holder of a first aid certificate.

A factor which VSO can never afford to disregard, and least of all in the recruitment and training of medical volunteers, is what the psychologists call 'culture shock', meaning the impact, on the individual who is accustomed to one environment, of the standards and practices of a wholly different one. To go, at the age of 20 (perhaps a little more, perhaps even less), from a British hospital or training college to a similar institution in the West African bush or the Bolivian *altiplano* involves a process of adjustment both complex and difficult. In the first place there are the superficial but never unimportant considerations of climate and diet; then the pressures of local attitudes of mind, occasionally hostile, certainly alien and unfamiliar; and finally there are the working conditions, both material and psychological, which may be disconcertingly different from anything which the volunteer has previously experienced.

How, for instance, do you prepare a volunteer for her first sight of India after the flight from England?

'The next part of the journey was shattering. We were met by the British Council . . . and driven to lodgings in the city, 16 miles away. On this drive I saw more human suffering than I ever imagined existed. It is impossible to convey in words such abject poverty.'

And what if this is not just something to be seen on the way in from the airport, but actually a part of the daily background to the volunteer's life? For the medical volunteers, less powerless than most in the face of such conditions, the shock can be the greater, because of the startling contrast between a bush hospital and the familiar pattern of life at Bart's or St. Thomas's.

'The dirt, the chickens accompanying us on ward rounds and the insects which drop onto sterile dressings do not worry us, but to find patients uncared for does. The students will not take the initiative and make a woman comfortable by washing her and giving her some water; one must always tell them over and over again with each successive patient.'

That was a nurse serving in Malawi, and her comments are typical of the reactions of others in the West Indies, in Malaysia, almost anywhere in Africa or the Indian sub-continent. And, of course, there are harder things to face:

'The main thing here [in Zambia] is the children – you could weep at times to see them. I've had a scrap of humanity brought in – Father brought her, complete with coffin. He had buried three children already. They died in Lusaka hospital, because they were taken in too late. He said burial grounds were 2/6 each in Lusaka and he couldn't afford it, so he brought the cardboard box ready.'

Medical work in the developing countries is most often an uphill fight against obstacles unimaginable in the Western world: purely medical problems are aggravated by undernourishment, by a total ignorance of hygiene, often by local prejudice and superstition – and always by the chronic difficulty of finding qualified staff and even competent assistance, both for the medical work itself and for the accompanying tasks of administration, supply and supervision. Distances are great, communications often rudimentary and unreliable, dependent as likely as not on the vagaries of the climate and on the ability of unskilled people to maintain and service whatever transport is available, from a Land Rover to a canoe with an outboard motor.

In such conditions, and where there may be a total lack of qualified indigenous staff, the need for outside help is unending. VSO could place with ease as many doctors as it could lay its hands on – but doctors who have recently qualified are pre-occupied, like the rest of us, with the need to establish themselves. It is not easy for them to set aside the claims of a career while they spend a year or two in the service of others, even though the experience they would gain by doing so might in the end out-weigh the material disadvantages. But even before qualifying there is a great deal that a medical student can do in circumstances where the qualified staff cannot cope with the volume of work. Given the basic minimum of supervision, there are many tasks which, in an English hospital, would be performed only by fully qualified doctors, but which can be delegated to auxiliaries if the alternative is that they cannot be done at all. Beyond this there is a mass of administrative and other work which a partly qualified volunteer can take over, leaving the qualified staff free to concentrate on purely medical duties.

This was the experience of two medical students from St. Mary's, Paddington, who went as volunteers to New Guinea. They had learned that medical auxiliaries were greatly needed, they felt the urge to escape from the confinement of a long academic course, and they were sure that in terms both of medical knowledge and of personal experience they would gain from a year of useful work in the field. Arriving at a modern hospital on the seashore five miles from Rabaul, they were struck at once by the excellence of its equipment and by the shortage of qualified staff – which helped to allay their initial diffidence.[1]

'At first we felt doubt of our usefulness because our medical knowledge was so slight. As assistants to the overworked surgeon and physician, each supervising about 80 beds, we gained insight into the local pattern of disease, learned the language, and then, more important, interested ourselves in the people themselves.

'After three months, because of shortage of staff, we were asked to run the outpatients and casualty department. At the start of this new role, the responsibilities seemed frightening. To admit,

[1] The extracts which follow are taken from an article which appeared in *The Lancet* on July 24th, 1965.

or not to admit? To which ward? With what diagnosis? For what investigations? These fears quickly vanished in the bustle of a department seeing about 100 new patients daily, of whom 6 might need to be admitted. When not working in outpatients we spent time following up cases in the wards and helping out where needed. The scope was almost unlimited; under supervision we were able to do a great many procedures . . . and the diseases we saw were as varied and (to us) exotic as the flora of the islands. . . . Clinical signs were very important, since history-taking was an exacting process, often involving two interpreters (there are more than 500 languages in the territory), and it might be quite useless, since the islanders often had no real idea of time or the importance of events.

'Apart from our work in outpatients, a number of other duties came our way. We found ourselves giving lectures on first aid and rudimentary tropical medicine. In the evenings we sometimes went with the Sister from the Red Cross Transfusion Service to stock the blood bank by collecting in the villages under the hissing light of Tilley Lamps. Here we saw and talked to the people in their own homes.

'For a time we found ourselves running outstation hospitals (of about 40 beds) as a result of staff shortages (in New Guinea the patient/doctor ratio is 25 times greater than in the United Kingdom). Here life was totally different, more what we had expected in Rabaul, and quite removed from anything we had experienced before. . . . We had to do everything ourselves – X-rays, blood examinations, gram-stains, tooth extractions, paying the staff, organising stores and supplies and, of course, ward rounds. Regular radio contact was maintained with Rabaul, and in a surgical emergency we could request evacuation of the patient by air to the base hospital.'

Trying afterwards to assess the value of this experience, these two volunteers stressed the amount of clinical material they had seen and which had provided them with 'a medical student's Utopia'; they were grateful (in retrospect) for the responsibilities delegated to them, which had greatly strengthened their self-confidence; and they summed up the benefit to themselves by saying:

157

'The amount gained depends on the enthusiasm put into the undertaking. In the situation we found it would have been hard not to be zealous. None the less, a previous knowledge of basic clinical medicine is necessary. . . . We feel that at least one clinical year should have been completed before such an expedition. We returned with a far greater practical knowledge of medicine, perhaps beyond the horizon of final examinations; yet the privilege of assisting in original field work, organising a medical patrol, or conducting a mass vaccination campaign are complementary to medical education.'

Finally, they were reassuring on a point of real importance to anyone who might think of following in their footsteps (and to volunteers in other fields as well), remarking that:

'The metamorphosis from the near "doctor-status" we were given in New Guinea to medical student again has not been as difficult as we imagined.'

Understandably, the medical schools are cautious in their approach to the idea of medical students volunteering before they have qualified. The arguments against it are clear: the disadvantage of interrupting a long and elaborate training programme, the danger of over-confidence in a student grown accustomed to relying on his own judgment in situations which would normally be considered beyond his professional competence. But the advantages too are unmistakable, most obviously to the countries which so desperately need the help which these volunteers can provide. Without it, they must accept a still longer interval before they can face one aspect of their development problem with anything like the certainty of success. And for the volunteers themselves, apart from the satisfaction that must come from answering the needs of others, it is difficult not to agree with those two young men in New Guinea that the experience and the assurance gained outweigh the cost of a year's delay in qualifying.

Out of 120-odd medical volunteers about half are nurses, and as a group they face perhaps the most exacting conditions of all. In many cases they are attached to small mission hospitals, maintained on the slenderest of budgets and holding their own precariously in the surrounding squalor and ignorance. I once visited one of these in Peshawar, at the foot of the Khyber Pass, where a London girl who had been nursing for four years at Bart's had arrived just at the outset of the fighting between Pakistan and India in 1965. When that was over, the hospital resumed its ordinary function of providing for the wild tribesmen of the frontier, who brought to it their sick as part of their twice-yearly migration – and stayed squatting in the courtyard, with their rifles and their cooking-pots, until the time came for them to accompany their relatives back to the hills. They were Pathans, proud, pale-skinned and remarkably handsome, resigned to the acceptance of suffering and altogether innocent of the principles of hygiene.

'The only way to describe the hospital' (the volunteer had written) 'is to ask you to forget everything you know about English hospitals and imagine a courtyard with little rooms all round it, rather like a stable. In these rooms are three beds and a locker if they are lucky. The bed linen is always dirty, because the patients are always dirty, even if we give them hospital clothes. I found this difficult to accept at first but now I see it more realistically. The predominant diseases are of the eye, T.B. and ghastly bone infections, things which I never saw in England. Most of the children have vitamin deficiencies like rickets and often malnutrition as well. And they just go on producing more and more children . . . Some of the histories are frightful – twelve pregnancies and only seven alive, and the mother has T.B. There are only three doctors in the hospital, two English and one Pakistani, so naturally the nurses do many things that doctors normally do.'

When I arrived, she was less than half way through her first twelve months; but already she had decided that she wanted to stay for a second year at Peshawar, and her resolve did not weaken when soon afterwards the hospital was flooded by the spring influx of patients.

'The hospital is very busy at the moment and I feel quite dead in the evenings. Patients' beds are popping up all over the place in the most unlikely spots and I'm told that we will have another 100 patients by the middle of April. Life in the operating theatre is hectic – about 30 operations daily. I found that it took longer to get absolutely au fait with the work than I expected, but now that I feel I am, August seems far too soon to think of going home.'

It was, I suppose, as hard a job as you could throw at a girl of 24 who had never been out of England before. She didn't romanticise it, and I fancy she would have difficulty in explaining to you just why she found it so rewarding. But she stayed the course and when the time came for her to be replaced by another volunteer, she wrote:

'Anyway I wouldn't have missed these two years for anything. I can't recall one single dull moment and I bet I couldn't say that in England in two years.'

Not every volunteer would echo that sentiment, and loneliness can aggravate the strain of hard work in depressing circumstances. This, of course, is something which VSO has to take into careful account, both in selecting the volunteers and in the choice of projects for them. The British Council, in its role as 'overseas arm', can sometimes ease the strain – but for the most part, however hard the work, it is the sense of meeting a real need that keeps danger at bay. From a remote dispensary in Zambia, another nurse, this time from the Middlesex Hospital, describes her first visit to one of the neighbouring villages, where she went to register the children and inoculate them against polio:

'I went along with one of our dressers to a village 12 miles away – quite a bit off the main road. We were scared at first that we wouldn't get any response. We arrived at the school, met the head teacher (and the headman) and got started. Soon . . . we ran out of cards and then out of polio serum. I thought they were going to crush me to death if I didn't get hold of more vaccine, so I came back and got our other bottles (for our next baby clinic here and the next village). By 3.30 we'd run out of vaccine – and seen nearly 300 children; and there were at least 50 I'd not been able to see. . . . Out of the 300 there were only two abnormal children . . . the mums only bring along their healthy children. Well, I suppose it's a beginning.'

Where only a minority of the population can expect to receive any medical attention at all, any kind of medical auxiliary is a rare luxury, and here again there is tremendous scope for VSO. Since the first medical volunteers were sent overseas in 1963, openings have been found for a wide variety of occupational and physiotherapists, radiographers, laboratory technicians, pharmacists and dieticians, many of whom have the opportunity to initiate something of direct practical value in fields scarcely touched in many of the developing countries. Ideally, these are posts where the volunteers can combine practical work and teaching, using their own professional equipment both to care for patients and to train local people to take their places when they leave.

Often the volunteers in this category are rather older than the majority, having behind them some years of practical experience – like the occupational therapist who had been running a department in Bristol for three years before she was posted to a busy hospital in Sierra Leone. Overcrowded and chronically short of funds, the hospital had a high proportion of mental patients for whose rehabilitation there was none to provide and who were the victims, as such unfortunates so often are, of local prejudice and inertia. Julia, who was 29, was invited to organise an occupational therapy unit and attacked the project with determination. She canvassed local firms for contract work which could be carried out in the hospital, seeking to give the patients an aim in view as well as an occupation; and she helped to plan the construction of a new building to house the unit, for which the Americans provided US Aid funds while the patients themselves provided the labour, reinforced by British and American volunteers serving on other projects in the area. Outstanding as an organiser, she found all the same that the African time-scale imposed itself and when the end of her year's service loomed ahead, with the job only half done, she asked to stay for another year.

In the second year the new unit was triumphantly completed and Julia started literacy classes for her patients, joined in the activities of a youth club connected with the hospital and developed the hospital garden, persuading the government to pay the patients for the work they did in it. She arranged for her Sierra Leonean deputy to go to England for professional training, and until the end of the second year she worked without a holiday in a climate generally reckoned one of the most enervating in the world. Political disturbances (by now it was 1966) left her unaffected, but more unsettling was a crisis in the hospital itself as a result of which the psychiatrist under whom she was working decided to leave. Faced with the prospect that the pattern she had worked so hard to create would disintegrate without her, she decided to stay for a third year – becoming incidentally the first volunteer to do so – with the idea of seeing the crisis through and holding the fort until her deputy was ready to look after the unit on her own.

This aim of continuity is a vital one if the work of the volunteers is to have any lasting significance. There is no point in starting something which will wither away once the volunteer has returned home, nor can VSO be certain – especially with the rarer kinds of professional volunteers—of finding a replacement every year. Even if it could, to do so would be to lose sight of the ultimate objective, which is to enable the developing countries to look after themselves. Having set the craft in motion, the next thing is to see that it becomes self-propelled as soon as possible.

A good example of this process comes from a project in Tanzania for which VSO was fortunate to find a qualified hospital administrator, a man of 36 with seven years' experience behind him at a hospital in the home counties. Posted to a teaching hospital in Dar-es-Salaam, Alan found the atmosphere 'fascinating, busy, friendly, exciting – and chaotic', and quickly drew up a report on how order could be brought into the hospital's erratic and confused system of record-keeping. To someone of his background and experience, the problem was a relatively simple one: like making a wheel, say, if you've been used to wheels all your life. But for anyone at that hospital lacking his experience and the habit of being systematic, it would have been as miraculous to devise an efficient records system as to *invent* the wheel. And to ensure that the trick, once revealed, was not lost again, Alan stressed in his report that a vital part of the reorganisation he proposed must be to provide the means of keeping the new wheel turning. Given the authority of medical records officer, he reorganised the records system, saw it established on a completely new basis – and personally instructed an African deputy whom he left in charge when he came home to England a year later. Alan, of course, was particularly well qualified to do this, being thoroughly experienced in his own field; but the principle is one which should apply to the majority of qualified volunteer projects, where the volunteer may lack experience but has the precious asset of a specific skill which can be imparted as well as demonstrated to those who have need of it.

For the most part the medical volunteers, like their colleagues in other fields, are posted singly to projects where they can supply some missing element of professional accomplishment. Sometimes a pair of nurses will be requested, who can keep each other company in some remote posting. Very occasionally there are openings for the few married couples who apply to VSO and who can only be accepted if each partner has some qualification which is in demand – like the two dentists, man and wife, who spent a year working for the Schools Dental Service in Sarawak, travelling from school to school and spending a week or two in each, and like other married couples who have served together in teaching posts in the same school or in two different schools in the same town. And now and then there are requests for teams of volunteers to tackle different aspects of a common project, like a trio consisting of a doctor, a physiotherapist and a laboratory technician who worked together at a leper colony on the outskirts of Addis Ababa. In every case the conditions on which they are accepted are the same: apart from the particular professional qualifications which are required, they must persuade the selectors that they possess the approach, the combination of qualities which is so much harder to define, which will enable them to make full

163

use of their skills in the context of this or that precise situation.

It is not easy to say just what this consists of, but it is illustrated perhaps most clearly by some of the younger volunteers serving in medical projects, though without medical qualifications beyond, say, a first aid certificate. At a small mission hospital in the Indian state of Rajasthan, for instance, a Scottish woman doctor working on her own was grateful for the help of a girl who could answer correspondence, keep accounts, mend a fuse, drive the ambulance, instruct the local helpers in elementary first aid and lend a hand with the countless other mundane needs– as well as the unpredictable emergencies – which harassed the doctor and distracted her from the essentials of the job in hand. For Alison, aged 19 and planning a career in social work with children, this was an extraordinary opportunity and she packed into her year in India a variety of experience which anyone would envy – but the underlying satisfaction of it lay in the fact that she was always busy, at tasks often unexciting in themselves but invested with significance by the tremendous need evident all around her and by the fact that her help made it possible to meet that need more effectively. She described a routine day like this:

'My day starts at 6.15 a.m. with a cup of tea in bed – bliss! Next comes breakfast, after which we all have prayers in the small hospital chapel. At about 8 I spend an hour in the office. There are always piles of letters to be written and masses of accounts to sort out. The rest of the morning is spent in the classroom teaching the nurses the practical side of nursing, i.e. bandaging, positions, trays, names of bones, etc. In the afternoons I am usually preparing for classes, writing letters or making board games for the patients. After tea I am usually in the hospital teaching patients how to make things for themselves. . . . I have now started a toy-making industry and everyone was absolutely thrilled when I produced a hand-made puppet – I don't think these village folk had seen a toy like this before. Anyway they are all making them now.'

Nothing remarkable there – and no mention of the time when the electricity failed in the middle of an operation and Alison repaired the fuse, or the night when the Indian driver couldn't be found and she drove the ambulance over the rough village tracks to bring an emergency patient to hospital – but it takes only a little imagination to realise the difference her presence made to the functioning of that remote outpost in a sea of poverty and hardship.

Medical, industrial and agricultural projects account for the greater part of VSO's work in the development as opposed to the educational field; but there remains an intriguing assortment of posts which fit into none of these categories, though they require of the volunteers who fill them the same general characteristics and inclinations. And here it is worth remarking that while the great majority of the volunteers are between 18 and 25, there is no upper age limit and no reason, from VSO's point of view, why those of any age should not offer themselves as candidates. In the countries where volunteers serve, the climate is often exacting and the living conditions, as we have seen, are seldom luxurious; but for anyone who is undeterred by these – and fit enough to withstand them – age is certainly no barrier, and experience an obvious advantage.

To emphasise the point there is the example of Ivy H., who retired at 60 after seventeen years as a librarian in Castleford in the West Riding of Yorkshire and decided that she had reached the stage where she could tackle 'some pioneer work'. VSO had sent its first librarian-volunteer to Tanzania at the beginning of 1966 and gladly snapped up Ivy later in that year for a similar post in Zambia. Here she began by training a group of assistant librarians in Lusaka and then took to the road to establish a chain of libraries with the backing of the UN Economic Commission for Africa. Eager and active, she was soon spending half of each week on tour and as the number of libraries under her administration grew she found the work so absorbing that she extended her stay into 1968, to enable a class of librarians to complete their final examinations at Makerere University and take over where she would leave off.

Librarians are among the newest categories of volunteers, and

165

there is clearly plenty of scope for them; within a year of the dispatch of the first, there were sixteen librarians serving in eleven different countries. Here is one aspect of the struggle throughout the developing world to establish the basis for technical advance – and there is an even more fundamental aspect in the world-wide campaign against illiteracy. A leading authority[1] on the subject has remarked that 'a country which achieves universal literacy is at once lifted into a new social, economic and political dimension' and has pointed to the example of the Soviet Union, where at the time of the revolution 85% of the population were unable to read or write. 'The new government', he observes, 'assigned top priority to the complete eradication of illiteracy. It took twenty years to do it, but it was done, with the results we see today.' It is estimated that there are now 700 million people in the world – two-fifths of the world's population – who are wholly illiterate, and most of them are concentrated in Asia, Africa and South America. Few of their governments have the resources to mount a campaign on the scale required and here again is an area of technical aid in which volunteers can reinforce the efforts which ought to be, and in some cases are being, made. Again, Zambia is one of the countries trying to tackle this problem and the 1966 report of the Adult Literacy Programme in Zambia paid this tribute to the help which VSO had provided: 'It is no exaggeration to say that without their volunteers, of whom there are now three, the Programme could not possibly have been launched so early or so comprehensively.'

For the volunteers this kind of work has a dual appeal, as one of them found who spent an absorbing year with the Programme between leaving Cheadle Hulme School and going up to Oxford. He stressed the stimulus of working for an objective of such positive value, something that met such an evident need; and he found it exhilarating to spend so much of his time on tour in the African bush, where, even if he had wanted to, he could not avoid making real contact with a society of endless interest to him. In quite a different context, the same sort of opportunity came the

[1] Sir Charles Jeffries, author of *Illiteracy: a world problem.*

166

way of a boy whom VSO sent out to the Trucial Coast, at the southern end of the Persian Gulf, where he found himself engaged in survey work in rough mountain country:

'My major task was to find a possible route for a road through the mountains, which were a formidable barrier to east–west travel. This involved a five-day aerial survey, using a British army helicopter, and almost three months of walking through the mountains sizing up the pros and cons of road construction over each possible route. I found that I was spending from three to five days at a time sleeping rough on the gravel beds of the wadis, and I grew to respect the Arab and to have an understanding of his culture and his perpetual struggle to live. . . . The thing that sticks in my memory is the terrific hospitality and friendliness of the Arab towards all travellers. Struggling to farm at subsistence level on infertile soil, he would always endeavour to send a traveller on his way rested and refreshed.'

Of all the satisfactions open to the volunteer, perhaps the most compelling comes from a sense of identification with some community poor in most things and in need, above all, of sympathy and understanding. Within a few months of leaving school themselves, many have found it, especially those assigned to youth work, among orphans in Bolivia perhaps, or the Chilean *abandonados*, the homeless ones, on the outskirts of Santiago. Or take the case of John D. – he was a police cadet before he came to VSO – who was posted to a leprosarium in Tanzania, 180 miles up-country from Dar-es-Salaam. Aged 19, he was attached as assistant to the Englishman in charge of the outpatients department; and when his superior went on leave, he found himself in sole charge of a programme of community development and rehabilitation which catered for the needs of 200 Africans, many of them partially disabled by leprosy. He became deeply involved in their problems – and found also much to learn from them:

'The African family could well teach us a few things. You very rarely see a mother punishing her children. Why? because there is no need, they always obey her. The elders' word is law to the younger folk. This was something that caused me a great deal of concern. How was I in my youthfulness to convey my hopes, ideas and plans to the aged members of staff? The problem was solved when Mzee Welah and I went for long walks and chats in the jungle, through the most beautiful scenes you have ever seen. Somewhere along the line we always came to some agreement which he passed on to the subordinate staff. . . .

'As my ability in the language grew, so did the bonds of friendship with the locals, and so did the problems. After returning one day in a jovial mood from the safari, I was met by my woodcutter. After exchanging greetings and news of the safari, I was staggered when he offered me his sister as a wife.'

Having negotiated this hurdle, and others, John buried himself more and more deeply in the life of a community far off the high road of the twentieth century:

'At Chazi the world went by in its own way. I knew nothing about the important matters of the so-called civilised world. In my world, today's problem, if not faced immediately, would still be there tomorrow. This is Africa. It's not swept away by the hectic pace which controls Western civilisation. My sense of values, which had taken my whole life to form, was transformed in a matter of moments. One was there in the situation itself and not miles away reading inadequate reports. Things which look so important from our point of view are not really so when we think about it. The most important thing in life is life – physical and spiritual. When you are in Africa you are caught up personally in the important life or death struggle. For instance, we planted our maize in January and watched it grow to the height of about five inches before it was completely destroyed by armyworm. Mr. Cooper told me before he left that you don't get anything out of African soil unless you pray and fight for it and over it. The battle of the land is vital, for in the land the people have their security, their hope and everything else. We could only plant again, pray, and *prepare* for the coming harvest.'

'To plant and pray and prepare' – you could do worse than that as a slogan for the whole anxious and inspiring process of development, which takes so many forms but whose essential purpose is to right the balance of inequality: inequality, above all, of opportunity. Sometimes, if you take the broad view and study the statistics and listen to the economists, it all seems a losing battle. But it's a battle we cannot afford to lose, and if the major campaigns must be planned at the highest level and fought out with all the resources of a technically advanced society, there is room for every minor initiative, every kind of commando and even guerilla activity, on the flank of the heavier brigades. It is here that there is a place for the volunteer: the builder, the teacher, the nurse, the librarian, the farmer – the list is endless in its variety and the only common denominator is the urgency of the need. Nor, in helping to meet it, is there necessarily any relationship between the importance of the work undertaken and the satisfaction it can provide. The criterion is the need – and the great thing is to be doing something about it. As Lin Yutang says, 'there is a greater pleasure in picking up a small pearl in an ash-can than in looking at a large one in a jeweller's window', and it is something of this attitude that underlies the happiness of so many volunteers in posts both obscure and uncomfortable, but where – perhaps for the first time in their lives – they can feel that thay have come to grips with reality. Like Robin, another jack-of-all-trades who worked among leper children in Zambia, supervising occupational therapy, keeping the records, attending to the mail, seeing to repairs – and whose pride and joy was the Boy Scout troop:

'I make no extravagant claims about that Scout Troop. They were a bunch of shockers as far as being Boy Scouts was concerned, but they absolutely loved it. I think that Saturday was the one afternoon in the week they all really looked forward to . . . their sheer happiness was uplifting.'

That was his 'small pearl', and it was the happiness of the leper-Scouts, along with much else, that made him say when he left:

'If I had hoped to do something satisfying, I had never dreamed of doing anything quite so worth while as this. The sixteen months I was there were a happy, hectic flow of days which passed with an amazing swiftness. Suddenly it was all over. Suddenly one was in an aeroplane leaving it all behind. It was all a memory, and the dominant thought was – how little one had done, how much more could have been done, and now it was too late. I felt a powerful sense of humility at the gratitude everyone had shown. . . . It all seemed so wrong, because it had all been so easy; it should have been me thanking them. . . . '

Chapter 10

Facing the Hazards

When the idea was first proposed of sending young volunteers overseas, the critics and the pessimists were full of gloomy predictions about the hazards they would encounter: the political complications, the diseases, the civil disorders, the social complexities – was it fair to confront inexperienced young men and women with all these, to send them out all unprepared into a world so patently at odds with itself, evolving so rapidly but with such an evident disregard for precedent or protocol?

Today it is easy to forget those anxieties, to accept the picture of the confident young volunteers bestriding the earth and coping equably with all the obstacles that nature or rude humanity can put in their way. The picture is not without verisimilitude, as we have seen – but the hazards have their reality, too. If they have proved less formidable to a generation impatient of earlier inhibitions, and have claimed an astonishingly small number of victims, it would still be foolish to try to romanticise the concept of VSO by disguising its attendant risks.

Broadly speaking, these are of two kinds. There are what you might call the external hazards, of war and natural disaster, of illness and accident, which one can guard against but not foresee; and there are the internal ones, whose danger lies in the variable human response to particular circumstances. To forestall and avert both is the difficult art which the operators of a programme like Voluntary Service Overseas must try to cultivate.

To illustrate the point, consider the case (happily an altogether exceptional one) of a university graduate posted as a lecturer to a college in Central Africa. From VSO's point of view he seemed an excellent candidate. Besides the technical qualifications which the post required he had travelled widely for his age, had helped to run a youth club and had shown initiative in finding himself employment during his university vacations. His referees described him as 'capable and conscientious' and the selection board, while noting a 'lackadaisical manner' not unusual in the youth of the nineteen-sixties, had marked him down as 'resourceful and anxious for a challenge'. Within a week of arriving in Africa, he tried to commit suicide.

The attempt was unsuccessful and after a short stay in hospital he was flown home to England, while VSO sombrely embarked on an enquiry which might easily have been a post-mortem. Every paper relating to his application was examined, without providing any key to the mystery – until the boy himself came into the VSO office after a period of recuperation.

He had been accepted by VSO during his last year at university. Then, after sitting his final examinations and instead of taking a holiday, he had filled in the two months until his departure by working on night shift in a hospital. When the time came for him to leave for Africa, he was mentally and physically exhausted and had begun to doubt his own capacity for the work ahead. The long flight deepened his misgivings and by the time he arrived everything that should have been a stimulus – the strangeness, the vivid sights and sounds of an unfamiliar environment, the challenge which he had sought – had become instead the cumulative elements of a burden which seemed at first alarming and presently intolerable. Before he had had a chance to come to grips with his task, his nerve cracked.

Once the immediate situation had been dealt with, through prompt action by the principal of the college and the nearest representative of the British Council, the problem was to decide whether this near-tragedy could have been foreseen and to use its lessons to prevent any similar situation from developing elsewhere. Just what were the lessons it provided, and how far is it possible to calculate the equation in which the principal factors are the personality of the individual and the nature of the situation to which he is to be exposed?

In the nature of things, the answers cannot be categorical. In this particular case, it is clear that the volunteer's own actions had subjected him to a degree of strain which was artificial and unnecessary; VSO cannot dictate the way in which a volunteer occupies his time immediately before going overseas. At the same time, the case did emphasise certain fundamental principles on which VSO has to base its operations. To begin with, it demonstrated the need for the most detailed scrutiny of every aspect of the candidate's personality. Secondly, here was another reminder of the need to match the volunteer as exactly as possible to his project, to pay close attention to the environmental factors (of remoteness, climate, degree of physical or social isolation) as well as to the technical requirements of a particular post. Two candidates with the same qualifications may be suitable only for very different projects, since the effectiveness with which they can use their qualifications will depend on the success with which they are able to integrate themselves into the local situation – and that in turn will depend on personality factors, which can make or mar an otherwise ideal project.

A third lesson concerned the briefing which volunteers receive before they go overseas. Whatever else they acquire, the volunteers must be given as clear an idea as possible of the situation that will confront them: of the nature of the environment, the standard of work required, the amount of cooperation they can expect to receive and the extent of the responsibility they will be expected to shoulder. Uncertainty can be exhilarating while the prospect ahead is still a distant one, an intriguing subject for speculation. It may well be unnerving when the challenge is imminent, when ability and character are both about to be put to the test, and in circumstances which even the most imaginative volunteer will scarcely be able to foresee. In this context the value of the returned volunteer as an element in VSO's briefing programme is clear;

only an old hand, someone who has actually served in a given situation, or one very similar to it, can provide the kind of detailed information which will strengthen and reassure the novice, buttressing his enthusiasm with the solid reinforcement of personal experience.

The novice, especially the kind of novice who signs up with VSO, is likely to underrate the sheer force of loneliness: not the absolute loneliness which consists in a literal absence of other people (for very few volunteers go to situations where this would apply) but the more insidious loneliness which can result from a sense of exclusion, of isolation in a sea of alien and possibly unsympathetic humanity. This can strike unpredictably, perhaps even at the moment of departure, as it did for one unusually self-reliant young man setting out for New Guinea (though in his case it didn't last long):

'Leaving England for a year was a miserable experience. I left with a thousand misgivings and feeling very sorry for myself – almost solely due to the abrupt breaking of personal ties. It was consoling that it was blowing a gale and the rain was pouring down at London airport, knowing that at least I'd have a year away from the bloody English weather. However, I had never been in an aircraft before and the 15,000 miles straight off gave me ample time to get used to it; from the moment we took off, I am almost ashamed to say, I hardly cast another thought back.'

Most volunteers travel out to their projects in charter flights, which give them the company of their colleagues at least until they set foot on a foreign shore; but at some point the moment of truth arrives. You don't have to travel to the other end of the world to feel isolated, as this graduate volunteer explained soon after his arrival at a remote post in the Sudan:

'I'm sure you will appreciate that the atmosphere here is difficult to communicate. My first reactions were ones of shock and horror. I must admit that for two pins I would have walked straight out at any time in the first two weeks; this place seemed the "end of the world" – the sort of area one imagines ought to be abandoned completely to the sun and the vultures. Insect bites, diarrhoea and sunburn didn't help and the food was terrible. However . . . the ease with which one adapts is amazing, but the hardest thing to swallow was the isolation. It's very easy to think that the life of the world and the centre of events is 5000 miles away.'

Sometimes the problem can be the other way round. Once a person has made up his mind to a certain proposition and faced what seem to be its implications, he may be ready for the difficulties and possibly the hardships that are involved; but if the challenge turns out to be a quite different one, perhaps more and perhaps less obvious than the one he expected, this too can be disconcerting. Here there enters in a consideration touched on earlier, of the romantic image of volunteering, which may be wholly inappropriate to a post where the contribution required of the volunteer is simply hard work in a humdrum situation. If this situation is much like the one he has left behind in England, he may feel cheated, deprived in some way of the opportunity to prove himself and deflated by the very absence of the obstacles he counted on overcoming. Of a graduate who failed to settle down to a university post in Ghana, one of his colleagues wrote:

'I got the impression that he was not prepared to meet people who dressed and talked and lived a life fairly similar to Europeans. He would have been much happier if there had been a sparse population of noble savages a l'anglais, and the rest of the country entirely populated with giraffes and lions. The squalor and bustle of Accra make it a bit like living in a slum at home, and I think he didn't enjoy this. . . . We tried, rather desperately when we realised that he was about to leave, to arrange a trek to a Game Park over Christmas, but by then it was too late. . . .'

Here, clearly, there had been a failure of communication and, as a result, a volunteer who might have done admirably in a different context was wasted. Where this happens, the fault may lie with VSO, whose briefing of the volunteer must have been, if not inadequate, at least unsuccessful in correcting his preconceived notion of what would be expected of him; or it may be the result of a failure of imagination on the part of the volunteer; or a combination of the two. If the individual is able to adapt himself, the mistake may not be irretrievable; but the only safe course is to see that the mistake is not made in the first place – and that is not always easy.

Closely related to the problem of loneliness (which means as a rule simply a failure to integrate oneself with the surrounding community) is the question of the amount of responsibility which may be left to a volunteer. As a general rule, the record shows that the head of a project who hands over too much rather than too little responsibility is likely to get the best out of his volunteer; but a volunteer (by definition and with few exceptions) lacks experience, so that there are limits to what he can reasonably be expected to handle without feeling the strain. Those limits were passed, for instance, in the case of a fifth year medical student from St. Mary's who was posted to a hospital in Papua, and had barely arrived when the only qualified doctor there left to deal with an emergency in the bush, saying that he would be gone for three days.

'He left me with a hospital full of patients, mumbling something about meningitis as he departed. I was flattened. Suddenly this was it. I was the only available "doctor" in several hundred square miles. Just as I started collecting my thoughts the local district officer came to a screeching halt in his Land Rover outside the house. Would I come to the radio quickly as one of the coastal outposts up near the border with Indonesia had a sick baby and the district officer wanted to know what he should do. Here I was faced with a radio – very confusing for the first time – and a patient I couldn't see, having to get an assessment of the baby through a layman. It turned out the patient was quite sick and had pneumonia. The next morning I was taken up the coast in the Malaria Control speedboat, 35 miles in quite rough seas, to fetch the child and bring it back to the hospital. He got better and indeed was my first cure. I must admit I felt very proud of that a few days later.'

A happy ending (which was only the beginning of a remarkable year of adventurous independence) – but a situation which caused

VSO to insist that no more volunteers could be sent to this project until proper qualified supervision could be guaranteed. This ruling reflected no sort of doubts about a volunteer who proved more than equal to whatever came his way. It was a restatement of the premiss that a volunteer has his proper sphere and level of activity, and will function best at that level and no other. To expect more or less of him than he is equipped to give – however willing he may be, and however exhilarating he may find the giving – is to misuse him and to invite disaster.

'Disaster' sounds like an exaggeration, until one considers the consequences (for himself as well as for others) of putting a medical student in the shoes of a doctor, where one false diagnosis could cause a tragedy which would haunt his subsequent career; or of subjecting a volunteer to the strains which so nearly drove that boy to suicide in Central Africa. But a less dramatic denouement could still amount to disaster in terms of the blow to the self-confidence of a volunteer placed in a situation to which he or she is unequal. To speak in this context of 'failure' is generally misleading, except from the point of view of VSO itself, which must use its experience and the machinery which it has evolved to see that every volunteer is extended but that none is stretched too far.

VSO does indeed calculate its own annual 'failure rate' and subject the components of this gloomy statistic to minute examination, with the object of identifying the factors which are most likely to prevent a volunteer from carrying his resolve to a successful conclusion. The criterion of failure is that a project remains uncompleted and a volunteer returns to Britain before the end of the minimum term of one full year's service. On this basis (admittedly an incomplete one – but there is no other way of calculating it with precision) VSO's failure rate has remained remarkably constant, hovering around the figure of 1 % over the whole range of projects for qualified and cadet volunteers, male and female, in posts both academic and practical. The figure does not include those who may have to be repatriated because of war or political unrest in the countries where they are serving; nor does it take account of serious illness, or of domestic crises which might necessitate the return, for instance, of a volunteer whose father died and who had to take his place as the family breadwinner. What the 'failure rate' means in effect is that on average one in a hundred returns early each year because he has found himself for one reason or another unable to carry out the tasks allotted to him.

The reasons, of course, vary greatly and it would be rash to base firm conclusions on a sample as small as this; but there are certain more or less constant factors. Inevitably there will be instances where the complex process of selecting and posting many hundreds of volunteers will miscarry. Where the posting is impeccable, there are still the tensions which are bound to some extent to influence anyone involved in any demanding work, and which may be heightened by an unfamiliar environment, by food or a climate which impose their own minor strains. There are the difficulties which spring from inexperience, either in personal relations (made more complex by the contrast of cultural backgrounds) or in the political circumstances which may have a close bearing on the work of volunteers. And there is the ever-present fact that the volunteers have cut themselves temporarily adrift from families and friends whose demands it may not be possible for them to forget or disregard. All these can complicate a situation for which VSO – because it has created it – must remain responsible and with which the individual volunteer, perhaps through no fault of his own, may find himself unable to cope.

Human affairs are seldom simple and where something does go wrong with a volunteer project it is not always easy to isolate the reason or to put the 'failure' down with assurance to this or that precise cause. Going overseas in the first place (and possibly for the first time) to a situation envisaged perhaps with some exactitude, but still inevitably shrouded for the volunteer in a good deal of uncertainty, involves a certain effort of will, a bracing of the faculties, which is not so easy as it looks for any but the most self-assured. To leave behind a family, a group of friends, perhaps a fiancé, who may or may not sympathise with the venture and may indeed exert, either immediately or at a later stage, a distracting influence, calls for a measure of ruthlessness, a confidence in one's own judgment, which not every young person can command. Considerations like these may sap a measure of the volunteer's energy without his being aware of it, or undermine his assurance at the very moment when he has most need of it, to confront what may be the most considerable challenge with which life has so far presented him. Subjected in this way to a variety of pressures, it may follow that without the warning of any recognisable danger signal an individual apparently self-confident and inspiring confidence in others will unexpectedly crack, as a bridge will give way when the weight which it was designed to carry is exceeded.

Where that happens the fault lies not with the bridge but with those who miscalculated the amount of traffic it would have to bear or allowed that amount to be surpassed. VSO must try to calculate the pressures and to see that they are kept under control; this is the essence of the business of 'project vetting', the investigation of every project submitted, for which VSO leans heavily on the advice of its overseas arm, the British Council. But the pressures which the project itself will impose are only a part of the problem, and for the rest VSO must depend on the frankness with which the volunteer recognises and reveals the inner pressures which may limit his own freedom of action. In his application form, and at his interview with a selection board, he will be questioned in detail about his own circumstances. In particular he will be pressed to say whether his family, and still more his girl-friend, has agreed to his going; for here is perhaps the most dangerous reef on which an otherwise secure volunteer project may come to grief.

There is another aspect to this question of human relationships as they affect the volunteers, one which has a greater significance for the girls who now comprise just over half of the total number. The volunteer is asked to do a job of work and to establish a new kind of relationship with the peoples of the developing world. Of the two, the second is the more difficult task, not as a rule for lack of any welcoming attitude on the part of those among whom the volunteers live and work, but because it can never be easy – even with a wide experience of the world and its ways – to achieve a real understanding with people whose background and attitudes are at most points different from our own. In one sense, the task is easier for the young than for the rest of us, because the young are free from many of the preconceived ideas that inhibit their elders; therein lies the great strength of the volunteer movement in the field of international understanding. But in another sense the task is harder for those who must make their way in the confusing territory of human relations, without the benefit of even those unreliable landmarks which experience can provide.

Let us be more specific. Miss Y., a graduate volunteer of 22, is posted to a teacher training college in a small town in West Africa. Her colleagues on the staff are friendly but unaccustomed to the company of an Englishwoman and uncertain of her motives in accepting a post which even they consider as a kind of exile. Her pupils are mostly older than herself and in some respects more experienced. Outside the college the town has virtually nothing to offer in the way of recreation and there is no European community. This is a pretty representative teaching project, and a good one, since the post is one which it would be very difficult to fill with either an African or a contract European teacher (because of its remoteness and the lack of amenities) and because it offers the volunteer little choice but to try to integrate herself as far as possible with the local community. But how does she set about this? What exactly does 'integration with the local community' involve, and what should be her guiding lines in attempting it?

On paper, the answer is easy enough. Miss Y., apart from putting her best foot forward as a teacher, should first make sure that she establishes her authority with her pupils and then use whatever interests and aptitudes she has – in music, dressmaking, sport or amateur dramatics, for example – to win their coopera-tion outside the classroom. With her staff colleagues she should try to cultivate the sort of relationship she would expect to have with the members of a staff-room in any similar institution in England. And if the community outside the college should offer any scope at all, it may be possible for her to join in some sort of local activity, through a church, perhaps, or a hospital, helping to establish a library or to run a Guide troop, which will bring her into contact with other elements of the society in which she is living.

All this is easier said than done. To begin with, in the eyes of this remote African community Miss Y. – however she may see herself – is an alien, the object, it may be, of curiosity or suspicion or amusement. The atmosphere that surrounds her will be conditioned by memories of the colonial period and by contemporary attitudes over Rhodesia. The culture she represents will probably be valued more for the opportunities it offers of material advancement than for any inherent virtue or interest it may possess for the African mind. On the personal level it may even be supposed that she has come to Africa out of self-interest (the allowance she gets may seem little to her, but it is much by African standards), and there may be those to impute even more sinister motives. Any or all of this will confront Miss Y. with an uncharted minefield of potential misunderstandings, which it will take all her tact and patience to negotiate in search of that elusive goal of integration.

There are, for a start, the normal hazards which complicate human relationships in any society – aggravated here by unfamiliarity on both sides:

'I have two main problems now' (wrote a girl volunteer from Thailand), "wondering just how I'm going to be able to leave this next year and also – men. The town is full of some of the most beautiful women in the world, yet they think that I, with straight fair hair, blue eyes and a fair skin, am beautiful. Consequently I have boys, since departed to Bangkok, writing regularly and signing their letters "from the deeps of my heart", and others phoning. . . . One teacher has in all seriousness (I think) offered me a Mercedes Benz if I will marry her son!'

That gives a playful indication of some of the problems facing

Miss Y. She wants to be friendly, to win acceptance; but her overtures may be misconstrued, especially by her male colleagues or acquaintances, who will have as much difficulty in judging her intentions as she in interpreting their approaches. Confidence, on either side, can only grow with experience and while this is being gained Miss Y. will have to tread carefully, learning to be friendly without becoming familiar, to accept local conventions while still maintaining her own standards, to make allowances for others but few for herself.

Beyond these purely personal problems there are others which one might loosely call professional: the problems inherent in the function and status of the volunteer. Most volunteers, we have seen, are teachers; and even where they are engaged not in the classroom but in practical work of some kind, there will be an element of instruction in the role they are asked to fill. They are there because there were no local people qualified or available to do the work they have undertaken; and the hope is that by doing this work they will at the same time be able to train others to do it, or by their example to persuade them that it is worth doing. In short, they are in a position to exercise a certain influence in the developing countries, and to exercise it in a variety of ways. They may do so in the course of their teaching, or by the simple fact that they take on jobs which the local people have been unwilling to do; or, in the ordinary give and take of social intercourse, they may help (most often unconsciously) to modify attitudes which have stood in the way of healthy growth and development.

This again is dangerous ground, and the last thing the volunteer is encouraged to do – it is also the last thing most volunteers *want* to do – is to see himself as an advocate for a particular 'way of life'. (In this lies perhaps the most marked difference between the approaches of VSO and of the US Peace Corps.) Paternalism is out; indeed, it was in part as a reaction against paternalism that VSO was devised. The volunteer is not an apostle or an evangelist. He is an individual with a specific job to do and his primary concern must be to do it as competently as possible; any other consideration must be a subsidiary one. But this is not to deny the opportunity he will have – indeed, he can hardly escape it – to influence the hearts and minds of those around him. Miss Y., in her lonely situation in West Africa, and quite apart from her need to prove herself as a teacher, will inevitably find herself to some extent on trial as an example, possibly the only one her new associates have seen at close quarters, of English womanhood. Very little that she does will be unobserved and most of it will be subjected to critical examination and analysis. Even though she may remain unaware of the scrutiny or underestimate its importance, it is quite possible that months or perhaps years after she has left the scene there will be African girls explaining their approach to a particular problem by saying 'that's how Miss Y. used to do it'. It's a sobering thought, both for Miss Y. herself and for VSO.

But the problems that confront a volunteer are not merely those of personal standards or of professional effectiveness. If they were, they would differ little from those which face any teacher, though they would be accentuated by the youth of the volunteers and the fact that they take up their posts as strangers from another world. On top of these problems most volunteers must learn to handle others, which carry political overtones, since they pose questions and invite decisions which may imply criticism of the 'host' government or society. Misgovernment and corruption are not unknown among the new nations of Afro-Asia. The race for independence has not prevented stronger tribes from subjugating their weaker neighbours, and sometimes trying to exterminate them. Inequality between rich and poor is more marked in parts of Latin America than anywhere in Europe. How is a volunteer to avoid taking sides on such issues, or to achieve 'integration' into a society which openly asserts racial or religious discrimination, or accepts the elimination of political opponents, or perpetuates the subjection of women by retaining such practices as female circumcision?

Again there is a short answer, which can also be a facile one. It is: don't get involved – and as far as it goes, it is the right answer. The key lies in remembering the proper purpose and function of the volunteer, which is to serve as well as he is able within the limits of his own competence. But to leave it at that would be unfair to the best sort of volunteer, whose social conscience is likely to remain as sensitive in Timbuktu as on Tyneside, and who will feel it just as urgent to combat insincerity or injustice in his new environment as in the one he has left behind. It would be wrong to ask him to countenance known evils or to turn a blind eye to others whose existence he suspects; nor, if it did so, could VSO escape the accusation that it was failing to meet its responsibilities in full. For the fact is that the volunteers, or many of them, are going to become involved, and for the best of reasons, in everything that will be going on around them. Non-alignment may be splendid as an abstraction, an ideal, but as a plan of action it is not always going to be practicable for energetic individuals who find themselves at the heart of events, and in whom detachment is likely to be interpreted by their nearest neighbours as a kind of disloyalty.

Then again, it is a part of the volunteer's purpose to influence those whom he goes to serve, to alter their approach to life and help them to develop attitudes which will enable them to break out of the limitations of their environment. To do this involves a kind of partisanship, an alignment with methods or causes in themselves good and beneficial. The real question is how to express this alignment, whether it be alignment with a community or an individual, or with a set of concepts, a philosophy of life. To take a mundane example, it is not uncommon to find in the developing countries a preference for the theory rather than the practice of the dignity of labour. To get one's hands dirty is not a general aspiration, and this complicates the task of a volunteer whose job it is to train mechanical engineers. To get over the difficulty there are, broadly speaking, two possible methods of approach. One is to urge the pupils, to wheedle and coax and exhort them, to forget their inhibitions and get to work. The other is for the volunteer himself to roll up his sleeves and show the way. One of the most successful volunteers I have encountered I first met flat on his back under a partially dismembered Land

Rover in Tripoli, whence his grease-stained face emerged to greet me. By the time that young man left Tripoli he was a demigod to some twenty or thirty young Libyans – and what was more to the point, they knew the insides of a Land Rover like the backs of their own hands.

All this, of course, has little or nothing to do with politics; but the point is that example can achieve far more than exhortation in overcoming established attitudes. And if this is true of encouraging reluctant young Arabs to dirty their hands, it is also true of any attempt to guide the aspirations of a community into new and unpopular paths. To criticise, to denounce, to condemn an existing pattern of behaviour is impolitic as well as impolite. It may invite the opposite reaction from the one which is intended; it is almost certain to render the critic unpopular, especially if he be a foreigner, and a young one at that. But unostentatiously to demonstrate a different pattern, one which can be seen to produce more satisfactory results, has a better chance of attaining the end in view (though perhaps not at once) and is less likely to produce a breach of relations.

On another plane the atmosphere of the Moslem world presents special problems, and particular opportunities, too, for girl volunteers. Teaching, as many of them have done, in secondary schools in remote provincial towns in the Sudan, these girls (all university graduates) have had no choice but to accept the restrictions of the Moslem social code. That they would do so, and could endure the limitations this involved, was a condition of their going. It meant for some of them an isolation almost complete from anything remotely resembling the pattern of social life to which they were accustomed. It required of them a measure of restraint and self-reliance extreme even in the experience of VSO. But it certainly did not deny them the chance to affect, however slightly, the prospects of emancipation for the girls they taught. In sharing for a year the cramped social environment of Sudanese womanhood, these volunteers provided by their very presence a window on to the unknown world outside. Few of their pupils are likely to emerge into it, and probably not many would want to – yet; but when they themselves are bringing up a new generation of Sudanese youth, it is safe to say that many of them will adopt, perhaps without realising it, ideas and attitudes to which they were first introduced by those free-thinking young Englishwomen.

In quite a different and far more direct sense, politics can affect the fortunes of the volunteer serving overseas. The decade since VSO was born has seen more than a score of new nations taking their seats at the international table. Sometimes their independence was achieved in peace, sometimes not, and in many cases it proved only the prelude to internal disorders. In some countries volunteers shared in the exuberance of the liberation, while in others they found themselves caught up in the disputes that followed. In this context, non-involvement was of necessity a stricter rule and VSO could only hope to survive if it was carefully observed. Sometimes the outbreak of fighting necessitated a withdrawal, and then the British Council had another opportunity to demonstrate its value as the 'overseas arm', using its knowledge of the local scene to advise VSO in London of dangers impending, organising with tact and skill the necessary evacuation. The civil war in Nigeria in 1967 provided the largest single emergency of this kind, when 150 volunteers were withdrawn without mishap as Federal forces moved into the breakaway Eastern Region and the civil war showed signs of spreading into other parts of the country. On a smaller scale the same problems have had to be faced in other parts of the world: in the middle east, along the Indo-Pakistan border, in East Africa.

When this happens, the reaction of the volunteers is predictable. They are reluctant to leave, they are inclined to underestimate the dangers, they tend to see VSO and the British Council in the role of over-anxious maiden aunts. Each situation that arises has, of course, to be treated on its particular merits, but generally speaking VSO has to resign itself to this unflattering characterisation. If it is going to err, in a situation which involves the personal safety of the volunteers, it has to err on the side of caution. As we have seen, the stresses to which volunteers may be subjected are at the best of times considerable; no one could wish to add to them the kind of difficulties which one graduate of Hull University faced soon after he started teaching in Northern Nigeria:

'I didn't know anything was happening till I got up Thursday morning, heard no school bell, and was confronted by an Ibo with an arrow sticking straight through his arm. No boys came to school that day, except one or two of the northerners, who behaved as if nothing was happening. . . . We sent them home and then hid the ten Ibo lads in Class V who were living in the school, and waited. I saw six Ibos chased, hunted down and chopped to death by mobs of Hausas and Bihrims (a local tribe) just outside the school compound. The mobs looted the school up the road from us . . . but for some reason left us untouched. Lots of things happened that day, but eventually at dusk we got the ten lads in two cars to the comparative safety of the police station. . . . We got off very light here, the mobs didn't try and enter the compound until it was too late, the lads living in town managed to get to the police station, and we only had one boy killed (from Class III). A. J. (another volunteer) had a bad time of it, because he was living in the Ibo quarter and spent a night with two of them in his room. . . . Anne P. also had a hard time, as the mobs swarmed across her compound, killing and hunting.'

It was experiences like these, in the autumn of 1966, which decided VSO to withdraw all its volunteers from Nigeria when the civil war started at the end of the following summer. Many of the volunteers protested, some came storming into VSO's Hanover Street offices to protest that they had been in no danger and to emphasise, rightly, that the disruption caused by the fighting would make the need for outside help more urgent. It was an attitude that did them credit – but from VSO's point of view the volunteers themselves were not the only ones to be considered; there were also their families, and even the families of volunteers in other countries, who had a right to know what steps were being taken in Nigeria to deal with a situation which could be repeated elsewhere.

This raises the question of where volunteers should or should not be sent and what criteria govern their distribution. What about Vietnam, for instance, or Indonesia, or Egypt? Should communist countries be excluded from the programme? Is there a test of means or security or political stability which countries must pass before they qualify for inclusion?

Briefly, the answer is that volunteers may be sent to any country which fulfils three conditions. First, it must want them – for volunteers are not sent anywhere except in response to specific requests from the country concerned. Second, there must be a degree of stability and public security which can satisfy VSO (and this is bound to be a matter of judgment) that there is no exceptional danger to life and limb. Third, there must be some organisation which can assume responsibility for the volunteers in case of emergency; in the case of countries with which Britain has no diplomatic relations and where the British Council is also absent, volunteers will only be sent if there is some independent agency which can act in their place and is willing to do so. In the light of these conditions it would be difficult (at the time of writing) to envisage sending volunteers to Vietnam, because of the lack of security. There is no obvious reason why they should not go to Egypt (which has never yet requested them) and they may shortly return to Indonesia (where they served before Soekarno's confrontation with Malaysia), now that diplomatic relations have been restored between both countries and Britain.

The lack of diplomatic relations in itself has never been a sufficient barrier. When Nkrumah still ruled in Ghana and broke with Britain, 'very few people even noticed the break in diplomatic relations', wrote one volunteer, 'it has affected no one'; much the same was true of other African states which challenged Britain over the Rhodesian issue. Nor, as Britain's former colonies moved to independence, did individual volunteers find difficulty in accommodating themselves to the changed relationship. Indeed in more than one country they assisted with the transfer of power and perhaps played their minor part in seeing that it went through smoothly. When Somaliland, on the eve of attaining independence in 1960, held its first general election, a volunteer was asked to help with the polling arrangements at a village near which he was teaching. He found it amusing to be given a most friendly welcome by the villagers, who presented him with a live sheep – and then went on to record a 90% vote for the anti-British independence party.

The problems that face the volunteer are many and varied – and in overcoming them lies the reward. The most obvious ones are perhaps the least formidable; in the long run the slow, steady fight – often a lonely one – to make headway in some small corner of experience or endeavour may present a more exacting challenge than the brisk confrontation with more tangible obstacles. Either way, the qualities of which the volunteer has most need are human sympathy and patience – and with them a sense of humility, a willingness to learn as well as to teach, which can put the whole effort and its possible achievement into perspective. It was something of this that one girl expressed when she wrote, after teaching for a year in a boys' school in Sierra Leone:

'If you think you're going to drive back the frontiers of ignorance and poverty single-handed, you're in for a big disappointment. Any achievement is made through contact with a few individual boys. But this year has shown me that education is essential to the development of the emergent countries in Africa. To be a part – however small – of a young country's development is, I feel, exciting and extremely satisfying, and makes any "sacrifice" worth while. And after all, what have I sacrificed that I didn't want to sacrifice? And how much I have gained.'

It is more than modesty that leads so many volunteers to stress, on their return, their feeling that if VSO represents some kind of bargain with the developing countries, it is they, the volunteers, who have got the best of the bargain. Nor, to be paradoxical, does this mean that the developing countries have got the worst of it, for the fact is that the better the volunteer does his job, the more he is bound to gain from doing it. The satisfactions are various: for one, in Malawi, there is 'this feeling of achievement –

189

of doing something that I didn't think I could, something I didn't dream I'd ever have to do'; for another, in Nigeria, the awareness that 'the jobs we're given to do here are such as we wouldn't be trusted with for another ten years at home'; a third feels that his experience in India 'puts that small island that you live on firmly into perspective, and whilst this country often exasperates I think we could do with a few VSOs from here to teach us what to value in life'. A sense of values; an understanding of the colour problem; emancipation from all kinds of factors which limit our own development and our comprehension of the world about us; above all, perhaps a measure of self-knowledge – these are some of the rewards which were impulsively summed up by a girl writing from Uganda, who concluded:

'I have learned so much about life and people. I have felt so many emotions – and if I was run over by a bus I would have the satisfaction of knowing I'd done something on my own.'

None of this comes without effort, nor does the experience by any means leave every volunteer with the sense, or the evidence, of concrete achievement. For the fortunate few there is the tangible proof of a road built, an airstrip levelled and put into commission, a medical centre established or a library reorganised and restocked. For the majority there will be no such positive satisfaction but only a nagging consciousness of 'the petty done, the undone vast'. Yet if the problems have been faced and the frustrations accepted, there are other ways of deciding whether or not the time has been well spent:

'Looking back over the fifteen months I have been here [in Malawi] I find it hard to pick out either the best or the worst times, difficult to assess how much I have changed since I arrived and impossible to measure what I have achieved or left behind me. But despite this, I feel that such a happy year must have left its mark both on me and on the people with whom I have been happy. I am really sad to leave and rather frightened at the idea of returning to England where people are not always so ready to smile, so eager to learn and so friendly.'

190

A hint there of what one might call, in the jargon of the space age, the problems of re-entry, to which we shall return presently; and a reminder of the fact that happiness, when it is shared, is in itself no inconsiderable achievement.

Chapter 11

Public Support for VSO

VSO started life as an independent organisation, and so it remains; but it could not have developed as fast or as far as it has without a substantial measure of public support. The technique of ardent improvisation which in the summer of 1958 launched fourteen pioneers into orbit[1] has had to be modified to build the programme up to its present level of some 1400 volunteers a year. Side by side with this internal evolution, implying a change of method but not of purpose, VSO has had to establish for its operations a firm basis, of which the essential elements are a sound administrative machine, an assured income and a sympathetic attitude on the part of the public.

An 'administrative machine' is hardly how VSO sees itself; but the challenge it has faced, as the scale of its operations has expanded – and their diversity – has been that of adapting itself to the measure of an administrative task both delicate and complex. Unable to envisage its future with much certainty, VSO has never been able to represent itself as a career service. Those who work for it do so because they find the job worth doing and (perhaps this is another way of saying the same thing) because it involves dealing with people. Numbering now about sixty, of whom only a handful are over 40 years old, the staff includes a growing proportion of young men and women who have themselves served as volunteers and so bring first-hand knowledge to

[1] To be followed before the end of the year by four more.

bear on the preparation and placing of their successors. Others have been recruited because they have experience in the fields of education, industry, agriculture or medicine, reflecting VSO's efforts to meet the increasing demand for specialised volunteers. Most of them could be earning more in other walks of life and if they prefer to stay with VSO it is partly because the work offers them a good deal of scope for the exercise of personal initiative and mostly, I would guess, because of the personality of a director who has made VSO peculiarly his own.

Douglas Whiting, who took over as director after Alec Dickson had left in 1961, has been called 'that rarest of animals, an idealist with both feet firmly on the ground'. Like Dickson, he brought to VSO a lifelong interest in the wider aspects of education, and if Dickson possessed the drive and the obstinate enthusiasm to get VSO off the ground, Whiting had precisely the qualities of energy, common sense and sincerity which were needed to lend it stability, to strengthen its organisation without losing anything of its sureness of purpose. As a schoolmaster he had made his mark early, becoming a headmaster in his early thirties, and had gained unusually varied experience at home and abroad. In South Africa, and later as headmaster of the English School in Cairo, he had taught in multiracial communities, and at the time of his appointment as Director of VSO he was in charge of Cheadle Hulme School outside Manchester. To the gift of making others want to work for him he added the capacity to work himself harder than his subordinates. The post at VSO fitted him like a glove.

As part of the reorganisation which preceded Whiting's appointment a strong Council had been formed, under the patronage of the Duke of Edinburgh, to supervise the operations of VSO. The Council included men and women of distinction in every branch of public life, among them two of the oldest friends of VSO in Janet Lacey and the Bishop of Portsmouth.[1] Its Chairman was Lord Amory, whose public reputation as a former Chancellor of the Exchequer (and his private one as a wit) were

---

[1] Dr. Launcelot Fleming, now Bishop of Norwich, whose letter to *The Sunday Times* had set the original scheme in motion.

less relevant in this context than the fact that he had a close and practical interest in youth work. Soon afterwards Lord Amory was appointed Governor-General of Canada and until his return his place was taken by Lord Boyd, acting as interim chairman, who thus maintained the support he had given to VSO in its earliest days, when he was Secretary for Commonwealth Relations. As Treasurer the Council enlisted Sir George Schuster, whose energy, after a lifetime of public service, made him appear like one of the volunteers himself. And a powerful triumvirate was completed by Duncan Mackintosh, a business executive with unusually wide-ranging interests; as chairman of the executive committee, he was to play a central part in the period of rapid expansion that lay ahead.

As far as finance was concerned, the vital corner was turned in 1962 when the government agreed to provide 50% of the funds for the programme of qualified volunteers which was launched in that year. As the scheme gathered momentum this proportion was raised (in 1965) to 75% of the cost of a programme in which VSO collaborated with other voluntary societies[1] in recruiting volunteers for service in the developing countries.

To suspicious eyes, government money implied government control, or at least the likelihood of interference with the purpose and practice of the volunteer movement. In fact, these suspicions have proved groundless and neither Conservative nor Labour governments have tried to influence the committee which was formed in 1962, under the chairmanship of the late Sir John Lockwood, to coordinate the work of the various societies without interfering with their executive responsibilities. Each of them continues to manage its own affairs, with the Lockwood Committee (since renamed the British Volunteer Programme) providing a clearing-house in which ideas can be exchanged and common terms of service agreed between them. In addition, a Council for Volunteers Overseas, of which the Duke of Edinburgh

[1] At present, International Voluntary Service, the United Nations Association and the Catholic Institute for International Relations.

is President, acts as an advisory body for the whole field of activity covered by the overseas volunteer movement.

The government was interested in volunteers as part of the wider pattern of British aid to the developing world. The Labour administration which took office in the autumn of 1964 symbolised its intention to develop and reinforce that pattern by transforming the old Department of Technical Cooperation into a new Ministry of Overseas Development. One of the ministry's first duties was to bring order into a situation where 'aid' of all sorts, in the shape both of money and of manpower, was being administered in a variety of ways and by a variety of uncoordinated organisations. Experts and advisers were available to the developing countries through the diminishing ranks of the old Colonial Service, through the comparatively new Overseas Service Aid Scheme, through bodies like the Colombo Plan organisation and through Britain's participation in the special agencies of the United Nations. With all these activities now to be coordinated under the wing of one central ministry, but with the demand for expert help inevitably outrunning the available supply, the role of the volunteer was envisaged as that of an auxiliary or a stop-gap, who might reinforce the efforts of the expert, or provide temporary assistance where no more highly qualified person was available.

This raised the question of the place of the 'unqualified' volunteer: the school-leaver with his 'A' levels, the medical student, the whole range of able and enthusiastic 'cadets' who had given VSO its start in life, but who had no degrees or diplomas to attest their usefulness in the context of a formal aid programme. If the numbers of qualified volunteers were to increase (and they did so, rapidly, after 1962) would there still be room for the school-leavers – and if so, would it be right to expect the government to provide funds for this part of the volunteer programme as well?

Over this issue a number of old battles had to be refought, old arguments rehearsed – but this time there was some experience on which to base a decision. There was no doubt in the minds of those who had been concerned with the early years of VSO of the usefulness of the younger volunteers in a variety of situations.

There was no question of the benefits the volunteers themselves had derived from their experience – and there was a further argument for continuing the old part of the programme while expanding the new. The original experiment had been launched under the slogan of 'The Year Between', and one of the motives behind it had been to enable a boy to occupy himself usefully between leaving school and going to university. If the universities and training colleges were now to be the recruiting ground for the new type of qualified volunteer, what could do more to stimulate interest than the presence at these institutions of those who had already served overseas and could speak from experience of the problems and the satisfactions of this kind of service? Quite apart from their usefulness in the field, these younger volunteers, when they returned, would be able to sow the seeds of interest from which might spring a further crop of volunteers.

These arguments prevailed. VSO determined to continue to recruit school-leavers and other 'cadet' volunteers and the government, largely thanks to the firm advocacy of Sir Andrew Cohen at the Department of Technical Cooperation, decided to maintain its support to this junior branch of VSO as well as extending it to the programme for recruiting qualified volunteers. This put a firm floor under the whole operation, but it did not solve all VSO's financial problems. It left the organisation to find approximately one-quarter of its total budget – and as the number of volunteers increased, so did the amount of money that had to be raised from other sources. By 1968, ten years after the treasurer-bishop had been able to cast up his modest balance-sheet on a small piece of notepaper,[1] VSO's budget amounted to £783,000, to which the Ministry of Overseas Development contributed £587,000. For the remaining £196,000 VSO had to look to its other friends.

At a time when the public is bombarded with appeals of every kind, close on £200,000 is no inconsiderable sum to raise every year. In finding it, VSO relies on a wide variety of sources, from some of the great charitable foundations down to private indivi-

[1] See Chapter 4.

196

duals, and as far as possible their contributions are channelled through a system which gives the contributor a direct interest in a particular volunteer. This is the system of sponsorships, by which a livery company, an industrial firm, a town, a charitable trust or occasionally an individual pays a fixed sum towards the maintenance of one volunteer.[1] The advantages are clear, in that instead of paying money into an anonymous pool, the benefactor is able to see how it is spent. He can keep in touch with the individual volunteer whose service he has helped to finance, and can very often help to make his service more effective by providing items of equipment which the volunteer needs for his work. In return the sponsor has the satisfaction of being involved in the work of the individual and of VSO as a whole. And from the organisation's point of view, there is the added advantage that in this way a steadily widening range of people all over this country become familiar and directly concerned with the work that volunteers are doing.

This process is hastened by the spread of a network of local committees which represent VSO in every part of Britain. When he first conceived the idea of VSO and was wrestling with the problem of how it could be financed, Alec Dickson had the germ of this idea for giving the organisation a really broad base and strengthening it by contact with the widest possible variety of local institutions. At the time the idea was not followed up, but in recent years the Secretary of VSO, Gilbert Stephenson, has devoted a great deal of effort to establishing and reinforcing these regional foundations so that today there are nearly a hundred VSO committees strategically distributed up and down the country. While no two of them are quite alike, they all – depending on regional interests and variations – bring together leading representatives of the various fields in which volunteers are active or from which they are drawn: of industry, agriculture, youth work, the professions, and in particular of education. They are able to advise VSO on problems of recruitment and to suggest where to

[1] At present £250, which is approximately 50% of the cost of maintaining a volunteer for one year.

look when some rare type of volunteer has been asked for – a glass-blower, for instance, or a braille specialist, or someone with experience of fish-farming. They can supplement VSO's own publicity campaigns by organising local meetings and seeing that they are publicised in the local newspapers. Their contacts with local employers of every kind, besides enabling them to ferret out likely candidates, are often valuable when returning volunteers need advice and help over resettlement. Finally, as part of their contribution towards that target of £200,000, these local committees between them are sponsoring eighty-five of the volunteers in the field.

From the earliest days of VSO a number of trusts and foundations have given generous support – providing in particular a substantial part of the financial backing which got the scheme off the ground in 1958 – and in this category it is right to single out Christian Aid,[1] which has been closely associated with VSO from the very beginning. The partnership between the two organisations has been expressed in the administrative assistance which Christian Aid provided when VSO was struggling to build up its own structure, and in the number of volunteer projects which Christian Aid has sponsored ever since. These are mission projects in various parts of the world for which Christian Aid supplies the money and VSO the manpower. At present they number about 220, and from VSO's point of view they represent a subsidy of some £55,000, or rather more than a quarter of the sum which VSO has to raise from independent sources. In the same way but on a smaller scale, organisations like Oxfam and the Save the Children Fund sponsor volunteers working on projects in which they have an interest, such as a well-drilling programme in Bihar or relief work among the Arab refugees from Palestine.

Industrial sponsorships form another category, in which individual firms both find the volunteers from among their own employees (usually those who have completed an apprenticeship) and as a rule meet half the cost of sending them overseas for a year. The number of firms cooperating with VSO in this field

[1] Formerly Inter-Church Aid. See Chapters 3 and 4.

198

lengthens every year and includes every branch of private and nationalised industry. Generally speaking it is the largest firms which provide the majority of the industrial volunteers, since it is they who can most easily spare an employee for a minimum of twelve months. But their example is spreading steadily through industry as a whole, as the advantages to the employer as well as to the volunteer of this kind of in-service training become apparent. Since the industrial volunteer can be seconded through VSO to a project where he can exercise and develop the skill in which he has been trained, there is no question of his growing rusty during his service with VSO. On the contrary, the experience he gains – both in his own field of specialisation and in the wider aspects of human relations – can hardly fail to give him the advantages of a maturity based on a deeper understanding both of himself and of the world about him. Nor are these advantages his alone; they are likely to make him a more positive asset to his firm and a more dynamic member of our own developing society.

For the public at large the image of the volunteer remains a curiously uncertain one. In a world so dominated by the concepts of advertising, VSO has largely confined its own initiatives in the field of publicity to the likely sources of volunteers; if anything it has avoided the limelight, leaving it to others to praise or criticise the work it has been doing. On the whole this has probably been all to the good, since there is about the organisation a healthy absence of self-consciousness. But the press, which in recent years has taken a close interest in the work of VSO, has tended to emphasise the romantic element about a movement which is at some pains to concentrate attention on its more practical aspect. For the newspaper reader, the lonely pioneer in his mud hut has inevitably a greater appeal than his colleague with a humdrum timetable of classroom work in an African secondary school – but the latter is the more representative symbol of the volunteer.

This consideration has its importance, not merely in the interests of accuracy, but because the real need, if VSO is to realise its full potential, is for a better understanding of what it is and what it can do. It is not a school for adventure, nor a means of sublimating the ambitions of a nation for whom the frontiers of opportunity appear to have narrowed. In the widest sense it is an organisation with a practical part to play in the shaping of a new society, both abroad and at home. First and foremost it can help to meet specific needs for skill or knowledge or technical accomplishment in countries where these are commodities as urgently needed as bread or bricks. Secondly, it can span the ravines of prejudice or misunderstanding which obstruct the process of communication between the old world and the new. Thirdly, by offering them the chance to exercise their faculties and to develop their initiative and their sense of responsibility – in the interests of others – it affords a proving-ground for those who are likely to be the leaders of the rising generation in Britain.

If all this is true – and I do not think it can be seriously contested – then it matters less what view the average newspaper reader holds of the volunteer than that the employers, the education authorities, the powers that be in every sphere of useful endeavour, should realise the opportunity that VSO presents and the extent to which their own attitudes can help or hinder its full exploitation.

At this level VSO is too often seen as an unwelcome competitor, a rival – especially in the closely contested slave market for the cream of the university graduates – or else as a distraction from the claims of research work or of higher steps on the ladder of purely academic advancement. Obviously every case needs to be judged on its merits and sometimes there will be cogent reasons why an individual should embark without interruption on the next stage of a predetermined career. But it is certainly arguable that for the vast majority there is a considerable advantage in having a breathing-space between the theoretical world of the university or training college and the practical business of living. It aids the mental digestion and affords an opportunity to get the world into perspective. If the breathing-space is well used, it can add a fresh dimension to life, giving substance to frail preconceptions (or else demolishing them), furnishing some of the missing links of knowledge or experience for lack of which even the best education can leave a man sterile and ineffectual. And what better way could there be of using it than to exercise, in an environment of particular stimulus and challenge, whatever aptitudes that education has aroused or sharpened? What better preparation for a career based on something more than mere self-interest than to pursue for a spell, in the context of one's own inclinations, the interests of others?

The resistance to this idea springs generally from an ill-formulated notion that a year or two of service in the African bush or the jungles of Malaysia will prove 'unsettling' to a volunteer, on whom the ruthless demands of twentieth-century specialisation impose, it is implied, the necessity for an exclusive concentration on the matter in hand. To this bleak conception of the purpose of education – or of life itself – Emerson provided the blunt answer when he wrote that 'people wish to be settled: only as far as they are unsettled is there any hope for them'. Certainly there are problems inherent in the abrupt displacement of young people, at a crucial stage in their lives, from an environment familiar and reassuring to one which is in all sorts of ways strange, challenging disturbing, possibly even alarming. There are also problems, which I called earlier the problems of re-entry, about their return and reintegration into their own society. But the answer, surely, is not to seek to evade these problems, which are only the kind of problems, though in a specialised form, which confront anyone who tries at any time in his life to break new ground and to escape from the limitations of an easy routine. Is not a better way to try to solve the problems, to ease the transition and to make sure that the benefits which this kind of service offers, in the shape of an increased awareness of the world about us, are not lost but rather capitalised as much as possible? In this endeavour the universities, employers in every field (including, especially, the public service) and the press can help by promoting a better understanding among the public in Britain of what volunteering is about and what benefits it offers, both to the developing countries and to the volunteers themselves and the society to which they belong.

The public's attitude towards the volunteers is at present one of

201

somewhat uninformed pride in their achievements as these are represented in the press or in radio and television programmes. What is lacking is a sense of public involvement in an enterprise which, after all, is largely sustained by public funds. Nor need the idea of involvement alarm anyone who feels that already his generosity is over-stretched by the demands of the starving Oxfam child and the myriad other claims on his conscience and his purse. What VSO needs is not so much more material help (though that will never come amiss) as a more sympathetic approach on the part of the public – and especially of employers – to the work it is doing. If the objectives of VSO are worth while and the benefits acknowledged, then there is no reason why a year or two of service overseas should not be accepted as a normal and valuable part of any young person's career and a positive qualification for preferment and promotion. In some circles it is already so regarded, but in others it imposes handicaps which impair its usefulness and may discourage some of the best candidates from coming forward.

An undergraduate in his final year (and the same applies to someone approaching the end of any form of professional training) is on the threshold of a natural break in his life. If he has decided on the career he intends to follow, he will feel a natural inclination to get to grips with it – and if he is outstanding in his field this inclination will probably be reinforced by those who (with his best interests sincerely at heart) will argue against any detour which seems likely to damage his prospects. He will be reminded that any delay in seeking employment will lose him seniority and give his contemporaries an advantage over him. If he finds employment, but asks for deferment in order to spend a year or two with VSO, the response may be grudging unless he can convince his future employers (or unless they are already convinced) that this will enhance rather than detract from his value to them. If his chosen career is one in which the competition is keen, these pressures will be strengthened by all the standard arguments in favour of 'security' and the need to establish himself; or, if he is to join a profession which is undermanned, like the teaching

202

profession, it will be urged upon him that his services are needed at home, and that they may be better employed here than they would be in some uncertain venture overseas.

Now these are substantial arguments, not to be dismissed without examination. It is true, they take no account of the central purpose of VSO, which is to help to meet the need of the developing countries for skilled and sympathetic help; and the objective observer may feel that this alone seriously weakens them. But even so, the interests of the volunteer have to be considered as well as the good he may do; and as things stand it is sometimes true that those interests suffer, that he does lose advancement or seniority or an increment because he prefers to undertake voluntary service. It is a partial answer to say that the advantages he is likely to gain are almost certain to outweigh these disadvantages, that the dividend in the shape of experience and self-assurance should easily repay the modest investment of a year or two out of the full span of a working life. If they might not themselves put it in such cold-blooded terms, most returned volunteers would subscribe to that point of view. But much could be done to ensure that the balance of advantage is more decisively in the volunteer's favour.

In the first place, I suggest, it should be recognised and accepted practice for employers to allow deferment to those who wish to undertake voluntary service before taking up their appointments. This should apply to the Civil Service and in the academic world as much as it already does in many sectors of private industry. Secondly, there should be no question of a loss of seniority for anyone undertaking voluntary service, which should count within the professional context as a period of employment on secondment – which it essentially is – bringing with it all the normal benefits of pension rights and pay increases.

These are not, of course, the sort of considerations which count for much with the majority of volunteers – but that is no reason why others should not take them into account. If it is fair to think of the volunteers as the youthful spearhead of a movement which deserves to have the whole weight of public opinion behind it, then those of us in the rear can at least see to it that the mundane problems of the commissariat receive proper attention. It should not be possible for a girl (a qualified teacher, with several years of experience behind her) to write as this one did after an intensely satisfying year as a volunteer in Malawi:

'It makes me feel like writing to the managers of the school I taught in at home and telling them of the experience that teaching is here. It was because they thought I was wasting my time doing VSO that they wouldn't give me leave of absence for the year.'

That girl gave up her job in order to volunteer – and she certainly did not regret it. Others who have volunteered before entering employment in Britain have faced the problem of finding a job on their return and have sometimes met with the same kind of obstruction which might have dissuaded her. VSO encourages volunteers to try to arrange the next stage of their careers before they go overseas, but this is not always possible, especially where an individual decides to serve for two years – which as a rule serves the best interests of all parties. Here again a more accommodating attitude on the part of employers, a closer understanding both of the benefits of this kind of service and of the motives behind it, could ease the problem of re-entry and remove what is bound to be to some extent a source of anxiety for the returning volunteer. VSO itself is able to offer advice on questions of resettlement, and a grant to tide the volunteer over until he finds employment. The organisation has a widening range of contacts with likely employers, both through the sources from which it recruits volunteers and through its local committees up and down the country. But it is not in any sense an employment exchange for the returned volunteers, nor should it need to be.

The returning volunteer faces psychological as well as practical problems. If launching oneself into an alien environment requires a readjustment of attitudes and priorities which had not previously been questioned, so does the re-entry into a world which may no longer look so familiar. Nor is it only the world which has changed. Somerset Maugham was not alone in feeling that 'I do not bring back from a journey quite the same self that I took away', and the young volunteers, exposed for the first time to patterns of thought and behaviour which may contrast and possibly conflict with much that they had taken for granted, may well find the re-entry disconcerting. A public in Britain better informed about what volunteers are doing and more sympathetic to their aims and their difficulties could help a great deal to make the splashdown less uncomfortable.

The returned volunteers have their own organisation, the Voluntary Overseas Service Association, which exists not to protect their own interests but to further the purposes of VSO and to extend them into voluntary work in this country. Its members make contact with overseas students visiting Britain and try to make them feel as much at home as volunteers have done in many distant parts of the world. Organised on a regional basis throughout Britain, they are active in various ways in support not only of VSO but of other agencies for work overseas; and they have made a striking contribution of their own to the pattern of international aid, with a scheme to bring individuals from the developing countries to Britain for further education or training which they are unable to receive at home.

An initiative like this has an obvious value in a world most urgently in need of closer understanding between nations. And in a more informal context there can be few returning volunteers who do not in one way or another influence the climate of their own society, bringing to bear on attitudes long frozen by prejudice or misconception the warmth of a sympathy based on personal experience. One of them, at the end of a difficult year in Nigeria, wrote that his own feelings had been summed up by Teilhard de Chardin in his *Phenomenon of Man*:

'The journey was over, and I felt keenly how little, of itself, mere displacement in space adds to a man. On returning to his point of departure, unless he has developed his inner life – a thing which doesn't show outwardly – he is still like everyone else.'

It is this inner development which so many volunteers have tried to describe and which finds expression in comments like this

205

one from a graduate serving in Malaysia. Writing of what had been for him 'a wonderful and unforgettable experience', he groped for the changes he thought he could see in himself, and came up with:

'a general broadening of education, and knocking off the sharp corners, but also a growing awareness of values, so different from your accustomed sense, but equally justifiable.'

Awareness and tolerance – we can never have enough of either. If we value them, VSO offers a way of generating them and giving them greater play in the society we are trying to build.

Chapter 12

Volunteers and the Developing World

In 1960 the 'development decade' of the United Nations was launched with high hopes. The world had found its feet again after the destruction and dislocation of the war. The economies of the advanced countries of the West were booming and the idea behind the development decade was to extend the benefits of this expansion to the poorer two-thirds of the world, to bring the populations of the under-developed countries into the swim of world trade and progress.

As the decade nears its end, it is clear that these hopes have been disappointed. It is bad enough that the gap between rich and poor, between the privileged and the under-privileged of the world, has not narrowed but grown wider. What is worse still is that among the richer nations, on whom the onus rests to find a solution to this most urgent of the world's problems, interest has slackened. Governments have cut back their programmes of aid for the developing nations. Public opinion in the West, distracted by internal difficulties and disillusioned by the apparent instability of the new nations in Africa and Asia, has shied away from its responsibilities. Stagnation on the economic front has heightened the tensions in the field of race relations. Examining this melancholy picture, a leading authority on the problems of development[1] remarked towards the end of 1967:

[1] William Clark, Director of the Overseas Development Institute.

'The political consequences of a world divided into a dynamic rich section increasingly separated from a stagnant poor mass are incalculable but deadly dangerous. The economic consequence for rich and poor is the inadequate use of most of the world's resources – including human beings.'

These consequences are by now well enough understood – and yet much of the urgency seems to have gone out of our attempts to forestall them. It was Aneurin Bevan who said that the introduction of television would mean that people would be able to sit at home and watch each other starve; during the 1967 famine in Bihar his prediction came gruesomely true. In the first half of the development decade, while the national incomes of the Western nations as a whole increased by 35%, their contribution to the aid programmes of the United Nations went up by a miserable 1% a year. Nor was even this increase secure. In the middle of 1966, preoccupied by its own economic crisis, the British Government reduced by 10% (or £20 million) the amount it was prepared to devote to overseas aid; and when the Minister of Overseas Development was dropped from the cabinet shortly afterwards, the move seemed to symbolise the lower priority which was now accorded to the whole subject of aid for development. In 1967, for the second year in succession, the United States Congress enforced drastic cuts in the American Government's aid programme. In Bonn the Bundestag followed suit by lopping £27 million off West Germany's aid budget for 1968.

It would be absurd to suggest that the volunteer movement, for all its rapid expansion throughout the world, can reverse this trend. Yet there is food for thought in the fact that while governments retrenched, the public support for such enterprises as Oxfam doubled between 1960 and 1967. The will, it seems, is there; what is lacking is an overall strategy for the campaign which the world must mount against poverty and under-development – and in framing this strategy, voluntary agencies of every kind have a role to play. Their work cannot and should not be thought of as a substitute for the action which needs to be taken at a political level. What they can do is help to create a climate of public opinion in which such action is seen to be right and necessary, and to reinforce it wherever possible.

Looked at in this light, the volunteer movement does have significance, both for the practical help it can provide and as an agent of change within our own society. Past efforts to promote development have often been unsuccessful and much time and money spent on aid has been wasted, because the attitudes and conceptions behind those efforts were ill-considered. Anything that can help to improve them, to educate the givers as well as the receivers of aid in the best ways of employing it, must serve the interests of both and improve our chances of working out a development philosophy which can lend strength and purpose to future initiatives. To build up a reservoir of young men and women who have worked overseas and seen for themselves the problems that have to be faced must further this essential process of enlightenment; and this is to say nothing of the purely human factors which must enter into any attempt to alter the structure of our social environment. Here, too, there is a wide scope for the volunteer, equipped with some of the technical instruments of change, but untrammelled by the handicaps of status or seniority.

'Development means more than stepping up growth rates of national income. It means transforming traditional societies into modern ones; it means changing human beings.'[1]

This observation, turning the spotlight of the sociologist on to problems which have too often been considered the exclusive preserve of the economist, exemplifies the new spirit stirring in the field of development studies. If change there must be, what sort of change is desirable, or practicable? And before it is undertaken, what are the characteristics of the existing society and how far are they going to assist or obstruct the processes of change? Are they necessarily inadequate to fulfil the hopes of that society for a better and a fuller life? If not, where does the inadequacy lie and how can it best be remedied? These are some of the questions that need to be asked, and that have not always been asked in the

[1] Paul Streeten, Acting Director of the Institute of Development Studies.

past, before a rational approach to the problems of development can be worked out. They can only be answered when we have accumulated far more detailed information than we now possess about the structure of communities in the developing countries and in gathering this information, in testing its application to societies at different stages of political and social and economic emancipation, the volunteers – with their close and varied contacts at the grass-roots level – can offer a unique contribution.

Take, for instance, a volunteer project at an up-country mission hospital in one of the most backward areas of Zambia. The hospital has 135 beds and an attached leprosy settlement for a similar number of patients. In 1966 Oxfam was willing to sponsor a volunteer who could help in the social welfare department, visiting the surrounding villages to investigate cases of need and attending to the personal and psychological problems of the patients, including the sufferers from leprosy.

Lorraine G., a psychology graduate from Sheffield University, seemed well suited to the post. Although she was only 21, she had been accepted by a VSO selection board as a volunteer of 'exceptional maturity' and she went out to Zambia in the autumn of 1966. (She has since extended her service and at the time of writing is still there, having played, in the words of the hospital surgeon, 'a vital part in a pilot leprosy scheme'.) In a report to VSO, she described a visit to a nearby village from which a request for assistance had been received:

'When first you go inside it is too dark to see anything. Then the dim outline of the walls of the mud house become visible, then the logs of the smoking fire, the bamboo bed at one side, rags hanging from the ceiling, and finally the old woman in the darkest corner, her knees drawn up and her arms curled about her to cover her semi-nakedness. Her skin is sagging and faded to brown, as the skin of the old so often is; her cheek-bones protrude from hunger and the emaciation of age. I wait to hear from the people of the village who have referred this "client" the not unfamiliar details. The husband will be dead, or possibly divorced, the children dead or gone to town years ago; there are no other

210

relatives around, and she is too old to cultivate, or to look after herself.'

Satisfied that the need is genuine, Lorraine arranges for someone from the village to come to the Social Welfare Centre to collect a blanket, clothes and food for the old woman. On the way back she wonders what would have happened to this lonely creature before the Social Welfare Department existed. Is her plight a sign that the old social structure is breaking up in rural Africa as it is in the towns? Well-travelled Africans, she notes, have been horrified to encounter the European phenomenon of the old people's home; yet now that similar homes are being built in Africa, the need for them seems self-evident. The pursuit of higher education, the search for employment in the towns, are weakening the family ties of rural communities. It may be, she reflects, that

'Public Assistance is hastening this process by transferring the burden of responsibility from the family and the immediate community to the State. Certainly the growth of a Social Welfare Department is found to be cumulative: the more people we help, the more appear at our office and are referred to us in the villages as being in need, as the news of our work spreads. The question is, is Public Assistance meeting a need that was unanswered before, or one that was previously answered in accordance with the old customs by relatives and friends?'

To look after even one extra dependant, she notes, can be a struggle for a subsistence farmer, especially if his children can now go to school and he must find their fees or pay for the transport to get them there. The social welfare workers try to reinforce the old customs where they can and to get the villagers to shoulder the responsibility for their dependent relatives. This they are often willing to do and she suggests that perhaps

'. . . the old sense of responsibility continues strongly enough but is being expressed in a new way. There is never any lack of people in the villages to tell us about the destitute and to show us where they live. Many turn up promptly at the office every

211

month to get supplies for their ageing or ailing relatives. There is the young widower who travels a considerable distance every four weeks to get food for his mother-in-law, though according to tribal custom his responsibility for her ended when his wife died, particularly as he is about to be married again. And another old woman had a house built for her, and supplies of food collected, by an unrelated man of the same village. People like this still feel a sense of involvement with the "passengers" of society, while aware that certain material necessities can be supplied on Public Assistance.'

To accept relief from the state, she finds, is not regarded as humiliating, but as a modification of the tribal assumption that the incapacitated should be taken care of by the community, and on this basis she concludes that

'The Welfare State is probably more in keeping with the African social philosophy, which is non-competitive and non-individualistic, than it is with the Western outlook. From the pattern emerging in Public Assistance work, there are grounds to hope that it may integrate happily with, rather than supersede, the socialist customs of village and family life.'

The conclusions may or may not be right, but there is no doubt at all of the value of this kind of down-to-earth experience, gained not in the course of a brief visit by a highly qualified expert, but over a year (or better still two years) of unobtrusive application by a volunteer equipped to interpret the data at her command. Whatever the problems that have to be faced, whether of education, food production, social development, hygiene, technical advance, the first requirement is to understand the human environment; only on the basis of that understanding can the techniques of development be adapted to particular circumstances.

To shape the strategy of development is not the function of the volunteers – at least, not directly. They serve at the behest of the governments of the developing countries. Their place is in the ranks – and sometimes in the labour battalions – of an army whose higher command must be indigenous. They must never forget that they are (indeed, it must be their aim to make themselves) expendable, in the sense that they will have achieved their purpose only when they have made their presence unnecessary, when the inhabitants of the country themselves possess the knowledge, the skills, the aptitudes which for the moment they must borrow from abroad. And because the ultimate aim, however remote its achievement may seem, must always be to help the developing countries to become self-sufficient, VSO has to bear in mind two factors which must influence the disposition of its volunteers. First, they must never be used as a substitute for action by the developing country itself. Second, their numbers in any one place or in any particular type of work should never be so great as to make that country dependent on outside assistance for an essential service.

These two considerations influence VSO both in deciding the terms on which it should offer volunteers and in framing its policy of future expansion. The present cost to VSO of sending volunteers (about £350 each for the cadets and £500 for the qualified volunteers) represents the amount spent on recruiting, training and dispatching them to their destinations, together with such items as an equipment allowance, insurance and a resettlement grant for the qualified volunteers, to tide them over until they find work after their return. The cost of maintaining them in the field is carried by their 'projects' – by the school or hospital, the government department or the mission society for which they are working. By our standards, the amount of these 'local costs' is not great: VSO asks the local authority or project head to provide board and lodging for the volunteer, with a weekly allowance equivalent to 30s. in the case of cadets and £3 for the qualified volunteers. Sometimes, especially where government departments are concerned, the local authority prefers to pay a fixed allowance to cover all three, and for graduates this may run as high as £700 or £800 a year – or as low as £300. The figure is not important; what is important is the principle that the project should pay for the help it receives, partly because this emphasises the cooperative nature of the arrangement, but especially because in this way

213

VSO can be reasonably sure that a volunteer will not be requested once there is a local person qualified to do his work.

It is, of course, impossible to generalise about rates of pay and the cost of living in different parts of the world; but in many of the developing countries free board and lodging plus an allowance of £3 a week affords by local standards a modest affluence. In some it represents for the employer a burden which makes the volunteer by no means a cheap form of labour, and in these exceptional cases (for instance, in some projects in India and the West Indies) the Ministry of Overseas Development, as part of the British Government's subsidy to VSO, is prepared to pay most of the local costs. Otherwise the principle holds that the local costs are the responsibility of the project, which will thus have funds set aside with which to pay a local employee when a volunteer is no longer needed or if one is not available.

Nor is it possible to be categorical about the future of VSO. Since its inception, and especially since the introduction of the programme for qualified volunteers, the scheme has expanded rapidly. At the beginning of 1968 there were more than 1300 volunteers in the field and by the end of the year the figure should be close to 1500, more than two-thirds of them graduates or holders of other professional qualifications. For the school-leavers and other 'cadets', whose number has fluctuated around the 400 mark for the past three or four years, any further expansion looks unlikely; their number may indeed decline, as the supply of better-qualified volunteers increases, not from Britain alone, but from the many other countries which have followed Britain's lead in this form of overseas service – and, of course, as more and more citizens of the developing world achieve a comparable level of skill or education, and are able to meet their own countries' needs for skilled manpower. With more than 20,000 volunteers from a score of countries now enlisted in this sizeable international brigade, it may even be that the volunteer movement as a whole is approaching a plateau from which it would be unrealistic (and possibly wrong-headed) to look for any further advance. Already there are developing countries where 50% of the teachers in secondary schools are volunteers, those from several different countries often serving alongside each other. While this provides an encouraging example of international cooperation, it also masks a danger which VSO must take into account in its planning for the future.

In 1967 the civil war in Nigeria necessitated the withdrawal of almost all VSO's volunteers in that country. They happened to be the largest single contingent, numbering more than 170, and the majority of them were teaching in state or mission secondary schools. They constituted, in the words of the British Council representative in Nigeria, 'an integral part of the structure of Nigerian education' and their annoyance at being withdrawn was not the expression of their own disappointment – though that often played its part. It was due primarily to the fact (which their experiences had enabled them to appreciate) that in the coming year the always critical staffing problems which afflicted most Nigerian schools, and most schools in the rest of black Africa, were going to be made still more acute.

The danger of encouraging too much dependence on the help of volunteers (as of any outside assistance) provides the best reason for limiting their number in any one country or province of a country. If volunteers are available in apparently unlimited numbers there will be little incentive for the Ministry of Education, or for any other department of an overseas government, to forge ahead with ambitious plans for training local people to take their places. Now, there are few countries and few fields of activity where VSO operates on a large enough scale to make this an immediate anxiety; but when VSO considers its future, as it must do, in the context of the whole of the international volunteer movement, this becomes a more relevant consideration. In Nepal, to take an example at the opposite end of the scale from Nigeria, VSO, with only four volunteers in the country, can hardly feel it is saturating the market – until it remembers that the American Peace Corps has 200 volunteers scattered across this remote land, whose contacts with the outside world have been until recently almost non-existent. Two hundred may not be too many for Nepal; it may even be too few – but in any country the benefits of skilled help on this scale have to be calculated in the light of the effect they may have on local initiative. It is a point which the Peace Corps needs to consider more carefully than VSO, working as it does with much larger numbers; but VSO cannot avoid its implications either, and seems in fact to give it much closer attention.

It is a mistake, of course, where volunteers are concerned, to think only, or primarily, in terms of numbers; what matters more is the quality of the help they can provide. With this in mind, it may be that some throttling back may be all to the good for VSO. In recent years, with the demand steadily increasing and while VSO was straining to build up its programme for qualified volunteers to its present level (expanding it at the rate of 40 or 50% annually), there was little chance to stand back and take stock. If you want to overhaul a ship's engine-room, you don't choose to do it when she is steaming full speed ahead in mid-Atlantic. But the phase of rapid expansion is now past; any further increase in numbers is likely to be more gradual, and this offers VSO the opportunity to advance in other directions, to improve its procedures and to see if there are ways of making the help it provides still more effective.

Undoubtedly there are, and there always will be. In particular, the volunteers could give better service if they stayed overseas for longer and if more of them could be given some language training before they went to their posts. VSO is working towards both of these objectives; but in doing so it needs to be clear-headed about what it is trying to do. This is where the idealists have to keep their feet on the ground, for as Browning observed through the mouth of Bishop Blougram:

> '*We speak of what is; not of what might be,*
> *And how 'twere better if 'twere otherwise.*'

If the volunteers are going to play a substantial part in the business of development, there is every reason to try to equip them as thoroughly as possible for the job in hand; but there is no point in thinking of them as something other than what they are, or confusing their function with that of the more highly qualified and experienced 'experts' who must remain the back-bone of Britain's efforts in the development field.

Language training would be helpful to almost all volunteers and VSO already provides it for those whose effectiveness as workers depends on their ability to communicate in a language other than English. Many volunteers use their own initiative to learn the local language, and some (like the psychology graduate whose work in Zambia was described earlier in this chapter) even compile phrase books for their own use and that of their successors. To introduce language instruction as a standard element in VSO's general training programme is tempting; it would also be very costly and it might, as suggested earlier,[1] be hazardous in view of the last-minute changes in the posting of volunteers which are sometimes inevitable. But most of all it depends on the length of time for which the volunteers undertake to serve. If the term of service is one year (the standard term until 1967), even a month devoted to language training makes a sizeable inroad into the period in which the volunteer is available to work on a project – and this is one of the strongest arguments for extending the standard term to two years, which would bring VSO into line with the agencies supplying qualified volunteers from other countries. The idea is an attractive one; but it raises problems which deserve thoughtful consideration.

Within the British Volunteer Programme as a whole the tide is running strongly at the moment in the direction of a standard term of two years' service for all qualified volunteers. The advantages of this extended tour of duty are evident: the volunteer gains a closer understanding of his new environment and is able to work more effectively within it; he has a better chance to learn the local language and to grow accustomed to local attitudes and methods – in cricketing terms, he gets the pace of the bowling and learns to adapt his strokes to suit it. For the African secondary schools which form such a large proportion of VSO's projects,

[1] See Chapter 6.

and which have to contend with such a rapid turnover of local staff, a volunteer who can teach and who is willing to stay put for two years on end is worth his weight in gold. Nor is it only the project which feels the benefit; many volunteers, returning after one year, have regretted their decision when it was too late, and it is very rare to find one who stayed for a second year and remained unaware of the advantages to himself. John T., for instance, who taught for two years at a technical school in Sierra Leone, wrote as the time came for him to set out for home:

'Certainly I feel I've gained FAR FAR more out of a second year of service than I would from one. I've really got to know the pupils, and the people of Sierra Leone as a whole, in a way I never knew them 12 months ago. Now "ah able for talk Krio small small" (I can speak a little of the vernacular). I've enjoyed my job this year far more than I did last year, when it was a struggle just to keep my head above water. I've made friends in a way I never did in my first year. I think I know a little more about how people from overseas view England and I'm certain I have a greater understanding of the problems facing the developing countries.'

So far, all is plain sailing; but there are arguments on the other side as well. To begin with, there may be solid reasons why a young man or woman who is eager to offer one year of service may be unable to offer two. The reasons may be domestic or professional, and they are most likely to affect the best of potential volunteers, the ones already marked down by future employers who may be reluctant to spare them for one year, let alone for two; or those who have already embarked on a career and are making a calculated sacrifice in interrupting it to devote a year to the service of others. Again, there is the fact that precisely those categories of volunteers who are hardest to find – like doctors, or specialists in the branches of industrial or agricultural science – are those for whom an absence of two years is hardest to contemplate. If they are needed overseas, they are needed at home as well, and faced with the choice between volunteering for two years and not volunteering at all they may feel impelled to give up the idea altogether.

Trying to approach this problem realistically, VSO has settled for the moment for a compromise which takes intelligent account of the different pressures at work on the different types of potential volunteers. As a general principle, the organisation is in favour of two-year service and it is prepared to insist on it for certain categories of work for which the supply is equal to the demand from the overseas countries. The holder of a teacher's certificate, or the arts graduate, who has no teaching experience and nothing distinctive to offer in the way of an extra qualification, must be prepared to undertake two years with VSO or show some compelling reason for offering less.[1] The scientist, the engineer, the medical specialist – anyone, in short, for whose services the developing countries are so eager that they will consider half a loaf better than no bread – will be accepted for one year and given every encouragement to stay for a second.

This brings us back to a point made earlier, and it bears repetition because it affects the whole future of the volunteer movement. The volunteers, whatever their individual motivation, represent one aspect of our approach to the world about us. Their collective contribution to solving the world's problems will be greater or smaller according to the effort that we, as well as they, are prepared to put into it. Involuntarily, we are all involved in the work of VSO through the support which the government provides for the British Volunteer Programme, and if we think the objectives worth while, we have the power to make them more easily attainable. The employer can help by accepting a period of voluntary service as a recognised and valuable preliminary to a normal career. Education authorities can help by releasing teachers for a spell of teaching overseas – from which they are likely to return with a much greater potential for in-

---

[1] For some countries, where the academic year starts in January, the teaching volunteer – whose service normally starts in September – is also acceptable if he can undertake to serve for 15 or 16 months, thus rounding out the local academic year.

fluencing the minds of our own younger generation. University tutors and heads of departments can help by encouraging their most promising young men and women to get out into a world which needs them and which has much to teach them in return. The public at large can help, perhaps by taking an interest in the work of the volunteers through one of the local VSO committees now active in every part of the country, perhaps simply by trying to revive the enthusiasm which accompanied the birth of the development decade, accepting the implications of what ex-President Soekarno of Indonesia once described as 'the challenge to the well-fed and complacent West . . . simply to *pay attention*'.

For that, when all is said and done, is the essence of the volunteer movement which VSO pioneered and which now has its spearheads all through the developing world. These young people are paying attention to needs and problems which concern us all, which are indeed in a very real sense our problems, since it is we, all of us, who will have to bear the cost if they remain unsolved. The present travail of American society, where the most advanced, the richest, the most highly developed social organism the world has yet seen finds itself threatened with disruption from within, is surely a lesson which none of us can disregard. The same problems of social and economic imbalance which there distract a continent are present on a much larger scale in the world whose doubts and uncertainties we share. There may be all sorts of solutions which are in the hands of the politicians or the social reformers, and to whose preparation we average mortals see no way of contributing. But here, on the margin, is one line of action which we can follow, one modest, unobtrusive campaign to which we can lend our support. By itself, it will not change the face of the world. But it may help.

*　　　*　　　*

For ten years now the volunteers have come and gone, some six thousand of them from VSO in the wake of that handful of pathfinders in 1958. To mix with them before they set out and then to meet them again after their return is to sense the effect that this experience can have on their own development, with what layers

220

of assurance and understanding it can clothe the raw material of eager humanity. Not all of them will have left their mark, nor would they themselves wish to exaggerate the importance of what they have done. They have served, and most of them would say they have gained a rich reward in return. You get an idea of one aspect of it from Peter C., who tells of his leave-taking ofter a year in an Indian village near Lucknow:

'Somehow the conversation got round to my leaving. There was a silence as we all lay wrapped in our thoughts. Suddenly my "dada" (elder brother) blurted out "If only you'll stay I'll give you half my land". "And I'll give you bullocks", said another. "I'll build you a house, all pukka with a flush latrine" (the HEIGHT of luxury) added another. And in no time at all I was fully set up for life in the village. Then my "dada" brought an end to the shouts with "There's one thing missing, he hasn't got a 'bebe' " (wife). So after a quick census of opinion they'd chosen a wife for me and were busy arguing how big the dowry should be. I found I was worth quite a lot! After a long argument they settled on a figure of 30,000 rupees and my "dada" seemed quite happy (he gets the money). Again silence. Abruptly out of nowhere my "dada" earnestly asked "You will stay, won't you?" And there was nothing left for me to do but to walk out into the warm silken night under the stars, with a lump in my throat. They were still sitting there in silence when I came back. They got up one by one and left without a word, without their usual "Jai rain".

'Then having dysentery and diarrhoea, lousy food without any protein, a mud hut, flies and heat – then all these were worth it. All I can say is "thank you".'

Appendices

A. BRITISH VOLUNTEER PROGRAMME

Graduate and Qualified Volunteers Overseas 1962–68

	62/63	63/64	64/65	65/66	66/67	67/68
Voluntary Service Overseas	36	152	339	601	1008	963*
International Voluntary Service	—	24	35	76	112	101
National Union of Students	—	22	46	106	23	—
United Nations Association	—	51	94	96	130	75
Catholic Institute for International Relations	—	—	—	—	29	50
Scottish Union of Students	—	6	—	—	—	—

B. VSO VOLUNTEERS OVERSEAS, 1958–68

	Cadet	Graduate/Qualified	Total
1958/59	18	—	18
1959/60	61	—	61
1960/61	86	—	86
1961/62	176	—	176
1962/63	284	36	320
1963/64	349	152	501
1964/65	392	339	731
1965/66	453	601	1054
1966/67	486	1008	1494
1967/68	404	963	1367*

* VSO's total includes those volunteers directly sponsored by Christian Aid, i.e. an average of 200 a year over the past five years.

C. BVP VOLUNTEERS OVERSEAS, 1967–68
Graduate/Qualified Volunteers

	Voluntary Service Overseas	International Voluntary Service	United Nations Association	Catholic Institute for International Relations
Graduate and Qualified				
Graduate Teacher	603	62	51	28
Agriculture	112	3	3	6
Technical	94	3	3	2
Medical	118	15	6	11
Miscellaneous	36	18	12	3
Total	963	101	75	50

Cadet Volunteers

Cadet	
Teachers	256
Agriculture	46
Technical	50
Medical	6
Miscellaneous	46
Total	404

Graduate and Qualified Volunteers and VSO Cadets

GRAND TOTAL	1367	101	75	50

APPENDICES

D. DISTRIBUTION OF VOLUNTEERS IN 1968

Code: G.T. Graduate and Qualified Teachers
C.D. Community Development
C. Cadets

Country	Total	G.T.	C.D.	C.
Antigua	5	5	—	—
Barbados	8	4	4	—
Botswana	11	—	1	10
British Honduras	9	—	—	9
Brunei	3	2	1	—
Burundi	4	3	—	1
Cameroon	17	8	1	8
Ceylon	13	2	7	4
Chile	3	—	—	3
Colombia	6	3	2	1
Dominica	8	3	4	1
Ethiopia	9	—	4	5
Falkland Islands	3	—	—	3
Fiji	12	1	6	5
The Gambia	13	7	3	3
Ghana	119	85	14	20
Gilbert & Ellice Islands	12	—	—	12
Grenada	10	7	1	2
Guyana	27	16	11	—
Honduras	1	—	—	1
Hong Kong	1	—	—	1
India	106	50	27	29
Jamaica	43	14	8	21
Kenya	109	44	41	24
Labrador	14	—	—	14
Laos	11	8	2	1
Lebanon	3	—	—	3
Lesotho	5	—	—	5
Libya	1	—	—	1

P   225

Country	Total	Category		
		G.T.	C.D.	C.
Malawi	85	37	35	13
Malaya	37	22	15	—
Montserrat	9	2	7	—
Morocco	8	—	—	8
Nepal	4	4	—	—
New Hebrides	8	—	1	7
Nigeria	18	15	3	—
E. Pakistan	11	7	4	—
W. Pakistan	24	12	5	7
Papua/New Guinea	36	8	2	26
Peru	5	—	—	5
Philippines	7	4	2	1
Rhodesia	2	—	—	2
Rwanda	6	3	—	3
Sabah	7	7	—	—
Sarawak	7	5	1	1
St. Helena	4	—	—	4
St. Kitts	7	6	1	—
St. Lucia	5	3	2	—
St. Vincent	7	5	2	—
Senegal	10	—	—	10
Seychelles	5	—	—	5
Sierra Leone	62	50	9	3
Singapore	17	15	2	—
Solomon Islands	25	—	—	25
South Africa	2	—	—	2
Sudan	20	20	—	—
Swaziland	5	—	—	5
Tanzania	131	47	72	12
Thailand	14	2	3	9
Trinidad	10	3	3	4
Tunisia	18	17	1	—
Uganda	91	23	26	42
Virgin Islands	8	3	4	1
Zambia	65	21	23	21
TOTAL	1367	603	360	404

E. VSO'S INCOME

Year	Income from Voluntary Sources						Income from Government Funds		
	Christian Aid	Local committees	Industrial companies	Covenants, donations, etc.	Voluntary sources (Oxfam, FFHC, etc.) through British Volunteer Programme (est.)*	Total from voluntary sources	Cadets	Graduates (via BVP) (est.)*	Total from government funds (est.)*
1958/59	—	—	—	9,573	—	9,573	—	—	—
59/60	4,460	—	1,400	18,408	—	24,268	—	—	—
60/61	7,650	—	4,550	24,300	—	36,500	—	—	—
61/62	25,850	—	8,400	6,514	—	40,764	5,000	—	5,000
62/63	50,400	1,400	11,200	26,923	—	89,923	15,920	—	15,920
63/64	77,650	3,190	10,000	78,191	25,833	194,864	40,000	46,620	86,620
64/65	67,750	11,600	11,500	78,795	53,630	223,275	52,343	90,400	142,743
65/66	52,000	15,500	13,250	44,411	30,400	155,561	86,331	216,200	302,531†
66/67	59,500	14,465	10,500	86,012	21,335	191,812	129,811	375,820	505,631

* Figures in these columns are estimated pending final agreement on allocation of funds within British Volunteer Programme, and audit.

† From and including the year 1965/66 the Government increased their grant from 50% of expenditure to 75% (within agreed ceilings).

Index

INDEX

Virgin Islands, 228

Volta Dam Research Project, Ghana, 146

Voluntary Overseas Service Association (for returned volunteers), 205

VOS, some aspects of work of: formal adoption of name, Voluntary Service Overseas Council, 1959, 51; first volunteers, 51–62; second stage of development, 62–3; early financial arrangements, 63–4; need for salaried staff arises, 64, 66–7; number of volunteers in 1959, 65; becomes independent organization, 67; for total numbers of volunteers, and locations, see Appendices; in field of education, 78 (*see* Education); prospect of graduate recruiting, 80–2; and the American Peace Corps, 74–6, 79; post-1961 insistence on qualifications, 76; Development section of, 77, 142–70; *see also* Medical, Technical; librarians recruited by, 165, 166; selection of volunteers, 84–93; training, 96–7, 99–100; growing emphasis on two-years-minimum service, 100; co-opera-

tion with British Council, 105, 116–15; supplementary training courses, VSO and BC, 113–14; public support for, 193–206; important factors governing disposition of volunteers, 213; costs of sending out volunteers, 213; costs to employers of volunteers, 214; future of, 214–20; present attitudes to two-year-minimum, 217–19; total numbers sent out, 220, and see Appendices

West Indies, 119, 147, 155, 228

Whiting, Douglas, 82; career of, 193

Wilson, John, 59, 60

World Bank, 32

World Health Organization, 13 n, 69, 72

'Year Between, The', 50–7, 195–6

Youth: post-war discontents of, 27–9; particular contributions of, as volunteers, 42–4

Zambia, 155, 165, 169–70, 210–11, 217, 228; Zambia Adult Literacy Programme, 165